ELIZABETH TAYLOR

ELIZABETH TAYLOR

Pyramid Illustrated History of the Movies

by
FOSTER HIRSCH

General Editor: **TED SENNETT**

PYRAMID
PUBLICATIONS
NEW YORK

ELIZABETH TAYLOR

Pyramid Illustrated History of the Movies
Copyright © 1973 by Pyramid Communications, Inc. All rights reserved. No part of
this book may be reproduced or transmitted in any form or by any means, including
photocopying, recording or by any information storage and retrieval system, without
permission in writing from the Publisher, except for brief quotes used by reviewers for
publication in a newspaper or magazine. Printed in the United States of America.
ISBN 0-515-03247-6
Library of Congress Catalog Card Number: 73-17970
Published by Pyramid Communications, Inc. Its trademarks, consisting of the word
"Pyramid" and the portrayal of a pyramid, are registered in the United States Patent
Office.
PYRAMID COMMUNICATIONS, INC.
919 Third Avenue, New York, New York 10022

(graphic design by anthony basile)

ACKNOWLEDGMENTS

The staff of the Theatre Collection, New York Public Library at Lincoln Center; Charles Silver at the Museum of Modern Art Film Study Center; Michael Kerbel at Audio-Brandon; Films, Inc. And a special thanks to Jerry Vermilye for providing the photographs for this book.

CONTENTS

In *Love Is Better Than Ever*, Elizabeth Taylor is a small-town dancing teacher. In *Butterfield 8*, she's a sort of model and some-time call girl. In *Secret Ceremony*, she plays a hooker on the skids. In *The Only Game in Town*, she's a lonely Las Vegas showgirl. In *Hammersmith Is Out*, she slings hash at a roadside diner. The rest of the time, she's just a woman, a non-productive member of a privileged class. Rich, beautiful, idle, she's a person of no accomplishments; her one goal, in movie after movie, is to get her man; her biggest problem is that she usually has trouble winning him or holding him.

The famous face and figure notwithstanding, Taylor in the movies is usually not good for men: she uses them up or steers them off their course. She's a menace to Vittorio Gassman in *Rhapsody*, demanding affection and thereby distracting him from his music. Her party girl in *The Last Time I Saw Paris* disturbs Van Johnson's concentration: with Liz around, purring and partying, he's unable to get to the great novel he knows is in him. The ultimate Taylor intruder is the Southern belle in *Raintree County*, a tortured, con-niving lady who detains Mont-gomery Clift in his search for life's true meaning.

ELIZABETH TAYLOR'S WOMEN

What *is* it about the screen persona of Elizabeth Taylor that gives her so much trouble keep-ing a man? Is she too pushy? Too idle? Too dumb? Too demand-ing? At one time or another, her characters are guilty of all these charges, but there's something else—some deep-rooted meta-physical lack perhaps—that dooms her to unfulfillment. Like many legendary actresses, Taylor has her secrets. *She* may know who she is, but she isn't about to tell all to us. The Taylor women, then, are always somewhat re-mote—that is their allure, but it is also their downfall. Men lose interest. Michael Caine strays from home in *X Y and Zee*. Rich-ard Burton is preoccupied with making money in *The VIPs*. In *Hammersmith Is Out*, Beau Bridges gets so bored with her that he wants to have her killed. An unlucky lady, Taylor often winds up with men who prefer other men. Marlon Brando, in *Reflections in a Golden Eye*, much prefers the clean, pure life of men among men to marriage with Liz. Cousin Sebastian uses her as bait for his boys in *Sud-*

denly, Last Summer. In *Cat on a Hot Tin Roof*, her husband thinks more about his dead football buddy than he does about her.

Ever the twitchy wife, the castoff mistress, the woman used and humiliated in the search for love, Liz has to work overtime to win the attention she feels is her due as the spectacular womanly woman she is. A very pre-feminist lady, whose only reality is the love of an adoring man, she's ready to sacrifice all for romance and (usually) marriage.

Many of the female stars who are in the same top-drawer league with Liz are independent types, determined women who know how to compete in a man's world. Crawford, Davis, Hepburn, Stanwyck, Hayward: these are ladies who have the self-confidence and the stamina to be executives, lawyers, heads of corporations. These manly women can and do make it on their own —*they're* not going to be demolished by the prospect of lonely nights. Taylor has never played an executive—the notion is preposterous—nor has she ever played an aspiring professional woman, a would-be actress, say, or a concert pianist. She never wants to *be* anything at all in fact; she just wants to love and be loved.

Straying husbands, misbehaving boyfriends, momentous amorous decisions—the Taylor women have certainly faced problems that confront the masses, but their world, encased in studio-created glamor and upper crust privilege, has been parallel to rather than identical with the *real* world. Often sincere, her performances are nonetheless a series of portraits of the Beautiful Woman as Movie Star. As Richard Schickel has written, Elizabeth Taylor "was, is and will forever be a movie star . . . since the age of eight she has had no identity but as an actress or, more accurately, as a public personality."° One of the last of her line, a remnant of the Old Hollywood and a studio system that has vanished, Taylor cannot qualify as a hip, modern woman; her characters, grasping and insecure, craving love and attention, are Tinsel Town fabrications, and Elizabeth Taylor in London or Ceylon or Texas or ancient Egypt or contemporary Manhattan is pure Beverly Hills. Magically beautiful, shielded by her fame and her money, she's never had a normal everyday kind of life—and it shows.

There are no gaps in the

° Richard Schickel, *The Stars*, New York, Dial Press, 1962.

public evolution of Elizabeth Taylor. From the little girl who loves horses and dogs to the nubile teen-ager, an expert tease who's preoccupied with prom dates and misbehaving boyfriends, to the rich young wife and mother presiding over Parisian town houses and Ceylonese tea plantations and monstrous Texas ranches, to the matronly shrew exulting in verbal clashes with stubborn, combative mates, Taylor has grown up in public view.

And yet the star who's held on to her fame for thirty years and who's enjoyed uninterrupted movie exposure has had the fate of most of the characters she's played: she has never been fully appreciated. Despite her fame and her unprecedented contracts, despite her Oscars and her nominations, she's seldom had a very good press. She's been attacked for her voice (a dry, light, high, sandpapery, lovely instrument), accused of lacking star presence and of coasting by on her face and figure and personal notoriety. She's no actress, the disclaimers say, she's just a broad with a face. And yet, surely, Elizabeth Taylor has not been an eminently bankable personality for thirty years just because she looks terrific and has had five wildly publicized marriages. No,

she has survived better than any of her colleagues from Forties MGM because what she can do she can do wonderfully well. When she's given the chance, she's a cunning romantic actress, a sharp-tongued minx, a deft comedienne, a *bona fide* siren. She comes out bland sometimes, impassive, but she can perform with flair and temperament nonetheless; she's her own person; she's *usable*. She can kiss and cry and bark smart answers with the best of them. Vixen, tease, bitch —she has a patent on all of these.

Her brand of bitchiness, though, is softened by vulnerability: Taylor always ends up likable. She's no "hoity-toity" movie queen, lording it over the plebeians; she's a nice lady who wants to please. The Taylor shrew, then, while she may sneer and claw like a tigress on the warpath, isn't finally a shrew at all; she's been weaned on courting audience sympathy in the last reel no matter what may have gone before, and so Taylor always ends up cuddly.

No meanie, Taylor's no rebel either. The stubborn Taylor young woman, leaping before she looks, is someone who has to be taught a few things; given the chance to make some mistakes, she softens and becomes, in the

final round, an obedient bourgeoise. In the minor but archetypal Taylor movie, *The Girl Who Had Everything*, she is the rebellious rich man's daughter who runs off with a romantic underworld type more appealing to her than the sober professional man her father has in mind. But when the affair sours, as it very quickly does, Taylor has the sense to get out and to return home to daddy and the rich, conservative life. As she almost always is at the ends of her movies, she's tamed. Nestled in the home with her man, the fighting spirit becalmed for the time being, Taylor is decidedly not among the movies' female rebels. In *Giant*, she cares about the Texans' mistreatment of the Mexicans, but she never really plays a Woman with a Cause.

From time to time, Taylor off screen was one of Hollywood's scarlet women, but she has rarely played a notorious lady on screen. Has she ever, in fact, played what you would call a really bad girl? She's never even been very wild. When she has to be a party girl, as in *The Last Time I Saw Paris*, she's too staid to be very convincing. Compare her B-Girl in *Butterfield 8* to Jane Fonda's whore in *Klute*: Fonda is tough and defiant; Tay-

lor just wants to get married, never mind sex for profit.

Tameable Taylor is not among the Hollywood neurotics either. She has played daffy characters, but basically she projects a robust, fun-loving sanity. On screen, she was locked up only once, in *Raintree County*; the rest of the time she's been among the sanest and steadiest of the big time stars. She's the perennial victim of romantic agonies, but, except when her character catches pneumonia (*The Last Time I Saw Paris*), she almost always survives. Like Maggie the Cat, Taylor's ladies are fighters, unwilling to stop until they get what they want. Her perseverance and her essential sanity are perhaps the secret of her endurance as a movie star. On screen and off, as young widow, divorcee, or mistress, outraging propriety and defying her elders, Taylor has had a dramatic time of it—but she's endured.

Fame and fortune have never sent her over the brink. A woman with a gutsy sense of humor and the gift of self-mockery, she's a corrective, both in the parts she's played in life and at the movies, to the popular legend that Hollywood destroys its own. Raised in but not destroyed by tinsel town, Liz has not gone the way of the Garlands and the Monroes. Neither an alcoholic nor a nervous wreck, she knows how to cope with the system that molded her. Obedient when it pays to be, but a fighter when necessary, she has the right sense of detachment to get her through.

Her critics, of course, claim that she's too aloof, bored with the movies because she's always had it so easy. Her life has been filled with romantic crises, but career struggles? Or battles for parts she really wanted? She never had to worry. She and her mother pushed fiercely for the role in *National Velvet;* the story goes that she willed herself into growing three inches in order to qualify for the part. But after that, the roles (some of them choice) have simply come her way.

As woman, the going has sometimes been rough; as movie star, it's been a snap. At the top at age twelve, she's stayed there ever since, thanks in large part to Metro's shrewd management of her career. The studio heads didn't always cast her interestingly, but they did try for some variety, and they steered her carefully through awkward transitional periods. From the radiant little girl in the horse opera in 1944 to the defiant, strong-willed big girl in the soap opera in 1960, MGM gave her gilt-edged star treatment. She was the prize package, the prettiest girl on the lot. The studio schooled and groomed her and touted her; a diligent pupil, she responded to the pampering.

Like her tinsel town persona, her movies are firmly in the Old Hollywood tradition. Animal stories, romance at the prom, cozy Main Street family comedies, ladies' magazine epics, teary dramas of domestic crisis—the Taylor canon is hardly strong on art or the conflict of ideas. Even when they have respectable literary antecedents (as they often do), her movies are in the popular mold: romantic fantasies geared to the masses. In that broad, popular, ladies' matinee range, however, hers is quite a decent record as Hollywood careers go. *National Velvet, Life With Father, Father of the Bride, Father's Little Dividend, A Place in the Sun, Ivanhoe, Giant, Raintree County, Cat on a Hot Tin Roof, Suddenly, Last Summer, Who's Afraid of Virginia Woolf?, The Taming of the Shrew, Reflections in a Golden Eye, X Y and Zee*—that's a thoroughly respectable movie-movie list. In her first decade in the movies, she was in some very modest programmers, mindless fluff for lazy Saturday afternoons, but since *Giant* in 1956, Taylor hasn't appeared in *any* trifles. There have been clinkers, of course, but each of the projects has had some charm or density, has attempted a statement or a technique that transcended the merely ordinary. And Taylor, as star presence, as international *femme fatale* or as aspiring actress, has worked with commitment and at least some sense of style.

Idealized in *A Place in the Sun*, the early Elizabeth Taylor represented a world of wealth and beauty; she is charming, responsive, reasonably bright, a good listener, compassionate. Travestied in *Boom*, the later Elizabeth Taylor is a parody of Hollywood vulgarity, flashing rock-like diamonds, donning garish portable tents, painting her lips and nails jungle red, cussin' like a stevedore. Either way, she is Hollywood's symbol of a movie star, she's the VIP who lives away from the world in barricaded mansions. As Angela, the symbol of untouchable perfection, or as Sissy Goforth, the symbol of cosmic vulgarity, as tremulous ingenue or as voracious Queen Bee of Camp, she is the privileged poor little rich girl, lonely, aching for appreciation, desperate for an anchor of security and conventionality among her world of the higher-ups. Seriously interested in being a woman, she is Hollywood's ultimate womanly woman.

In the making of the Elizabeth Taylor myth, art and life have always kept close company. On stage, as mistress or betrayed wife, Taylor was often part of a triangle. In real life, as we all know, she has twice broken up a marriage, stealing Eddie from Debbie and Richard from Sybil. Once a widow, once married to an older man, once the teen-age wife of the world's most eligible bachelor, twice married to burly types who gave her the protection she always needed—Taylor's private roles mirror her professional ones. Married to big business (Nicky Hilton), to splashy show biz (Mike Todd, Eddie Fisher), to protective Britishers (Michael Wilding, Richard Burton), Liz has usually picked up the personalities of her husbands. For Eddie, she became Jewish; for Richard, a lover of poetry. Because Mike Todd thought she was a "great little actress," she began to take her work seriously.

The movie image kept pace with the marriages. The shallow ingenue married an irresponsible millionaire's son. Nicky Hilton was more interested in gambling than in his new bride. (The role of the idle, neglected young wife is, of course, a Taylor staple.) Metro's prize teen-ager told reporters she was marrying Nicky "because we both adore over-

THE LADY'S NOT A TRAMP

size sweaters, hamburgers with onions and Ezio Pinza." After the short-lived honeymoon, a sadder but wiser young lady announced that "marriage is a lot more than a cottage with roses trailing over the fence." In one of her most quoted confidences, she admitted to the press that she had "the body of a woman and the mind of a child."

Marriage to Michael Wilding was much more sober. She played the well-brought-up young woman to his paternal man of the world. She tried, but Liz was too fun-loving to stay dignified too long. Mike Todd brought her out in a way neither of her previous husbands was able to. As a producer, Todd's motto was to give the customers "a meat and potatoes show. Dames and comedy—high dames and low comedy." The scrappy, nervy entrepreneur discovered the dame in Liz, and the ethereal former Mrs. Michael Wilding picked up some of her new man's brashness: the vulgar Elizabeth Taylor, the gal who loves to curse and to fight with her husband in public, was born.

With Michael Wilding and son Michael Howard, January, 1953

With Michael Todd

With Eddie Fisher

After the high-stepping, fast-living times with Todd, life with a crooner on his way down was slow. Eddie wasn't enough of a challenge. *She* had to be the strong one—and she wasn't well cast in the part.

But Richard, stable, a man's man (and a woman's man too), impressed by his own intelligence and culture, a protection against the outside world and a support within the world of show biz hustle, was just what the doctor ordered. It began in a flaunting of decorum,

Baby Elizabeth

but while it lasted, the marriage of Mr. and Mrs. Richard Burton was a study in wealthy, middle-aged respectability: Maggie the Cat got her Brick, Petruchio tamed his Kate.

Elizabeth Taylor in life found what Elizabeth Taylor on screen always yearned for—a real man to take care of her. Middle-class to the core, she was the dutiful wife, the concerned and sensible mother, the doting grandmother, the fun-loving but essentially respectable lady of leisure.

She was born in London, but Taylor's sensibility, her temperament, and her manner are quintessentially Southern Californian. Her father an art dealer with an office in the Beverly Hills Hotel, her mother a former actress ambitious for her daughter, Liz was brought up on the genteel fringe of the movie business. There are stories, not hard to believe, that agents approached Mrs. Taylor on the street, offering to introduce her remarkable daughter to the right producers. Mrs. Taylor held out for a while, feeling Elizabeth was too young to be thrown into the high-pressured movie world— but she didn't hold out for long.

Faced with offers from Universal and MGM, Mrs. Taylor selected the smaller studio: "We

THERE'S ONE BORN EVERY MINUTE (1942). With Carl "Alfalfa" Switzer

thought it would be better for Elizabeth." The little girl, though, was a flop. The studio put her into a modest screwball comedy called *There's One Born Every Minute* (1942). As the youngest daughter in a zany family that inherits the Tasty Pudding Company, pint-sized Liz sings a duet with Carl "Alfalfa" Switzer of the Our Gang comedies. Even then she was no singer, and she was no brat either—which is what she played.

The movie was dumped on the bottom half of double bills, but even more significant was the fact that the casting director just didn't like the child: "The kid has nothing. Her eyes are too old; she doesn't have the face of a kid." Yet it was those preternatural eyes and that wise face on the body of a child that were to be the making of Elizabeth Taylor. Even as a ten-year-old, Liz radiated the womanly wisdom and instinctive female guile that helped make her a star; Universal miscalculated in trying to transform an ethereal child into a

LASSIE COME HOME (1943). With Nigel Bruce

conventional studio brat who sings.

Liz was not used again for the duration of her contract, but by this time stage mother Taylor was determined to secure a place for her daughter in Hollywood. With the collusion of Mr. Taylor, she nabbed the attention of Sam Marx, the producer of *Lassie Come Home*, who was scouting for a little girl with an English accent to appear in about ten scenes in the virtually completed dog movie. Charmed by "the dainty dignity" of the Taylors' girl, he put her into his warm-hearted family film.

This time Elizabeth clicked. Her part was certainly modest, but the poised and even rather stately little "English" girl with the face of a woman attracted critical attention. MGM took notice—and we all know the rest.

MGM, the cotton candy dream factory, took good care of her. They used her sparingly, choosing roles in which she aged gracefully from radiant child to young woman. From *National Velvet* in 1944 to *The Last Time I Saw Paris* in 1954, Taylor was given the full contract star treatment, and she was an obedient student, listening to the studio bosses as well as to her vigilant mother. On the set, the omnipresent Mrs. Taylor would give her daughter hand signals. When the high Taylor voice got too shrill, Mrs. T. touched her stomach. When Liz wasn't delivering her lines with enough feeling, Mother put her hand to her heart. A finger on the cheek meant "smile more"; a finger on the neck meant "you're overdoing it." (Mrs. Taylor also saw to it, when her daughter was an unusually developed young lady of fourteen, that the girl wore clothes that accented the curves.)

For the pliant young actress, prestige movies mingled with Metro pulp. A programmer like *Courage of Lassie* followed *National Velvet; Cynthia* was the best vehicle the studio could come up with as a showcase for the teen-age star. But she was never used indiscriminately, and she was given the chance to play different kinds of young girls. In

HORSES AND DOGS

these early movies, she was both saint and sinner, both ethereal, untouchable and smoldering *femme fatale*. As little puritan or incipient vamp, the child with the grown-up face was magical.

In his famous review of *National Velvet* in *The Nation*, James Agee spoke for the critics who had a crush on the girl you wished lived next door. "Frankly," he sighed, "I doubt I am qualified to arrive at any sensible assessment of Miss Elizabeth Taylor. Ever since I first saw the child, two or three years ago . . . I have been choked with the peculiar sort of adoration I might have felt if we were both in the same grade of primary school. So far as I can see on an exceedingly cloudy day, I wouldn't say she is particularly gifted as an actress. She seems, rather, to turn things on and off, much as she is told. . . . She strikes me, however, if I may resort to conservative statement, as being rapturously beautiful . . . (since) I think it is the most hopeful business of movies to find the perfect people rather than the perfect artists, I think

At age twelve

NATIONAL VELVET (1944). As Velvet Brown

she and the picture are wonderful, and I hardly know or care whether she can act or not."°

In *Lassie Come Home*, *National Velvet*, and *The Courage of Lassie*, the young Elizabeth Taylor loves animals; in all her other movies, she loves men. As

°James Agee, *The Nation*, December 23, 1944.

horse-trainer or dog-owner, as spurned wife or mistress, she's a female who is absorbed in the giving and receiving of love: devotion to the object of passion is the center of her life. Little Liz lavishes love on horses and dogs with remarkable intensity, with, as Agee noted, "an odd sort of pre-specific erotic sentience." In

NATIONAL VELVET (1944). With Anne Revere

NATIONAL VELVET (1944). With Anne Revere and Mickey Rooney

The New Republic, Manny Farber wrote that "Velvet's love for horses is written past the usual insipid movie point for such childhood fanaticism, and is made to seem, sometimes painfully, like the real thing. Not only does she make you wonder uncomfortably what her motives are when she says she wants to be 'the greatest rider in the world,' but her favorite pastime is galloping over the countryside as though she were riding a horse and doing some more galloping in bed before going to sleep. Her passion seemed to me at all times more real than Bernadette's."[*]

Ecstatic, a dreamer with a turbulent emotional life, persistent, the young Liz dedicates herself to the prize-winning horse the way she later devotes herself to men. Anticipating her later images of young sex goddess and matronly earth mother, Liz as Velvet is both saintly and ripe. Howard Barnes, in the *New York Herald Tribune*, called her a child who "lights up with the integrity of a great passion."

Directed by Clarence Brown with loving attention to detail, the movie that made her a star is folksy family corn that deserves

[*]Manny Farber, *The New Republic*, February 5, 1945.

its place as a kiddie matinee perennial. With its picture-postcard English village by the sea, its rolling hills and thatched cottages, and its plain, God-fearing family, *National Velvet* is the product of a bygone era in moviemaking. Following closely the structure of the popular Enid Bagnold novel, the movie is part horse story, part family portrait: scenes of training and riding are balanced by cozy family scenes, vignettes about young love and sermons from Mom on the virtues of courage and endurance.

The Browns are a noble version of Hollywood rustic. Dedicated to a sober work ethic, they live quiet, exemplary lives. Mrs. Brown (Anne Revere) is the very spirit of plain-folk wisdom; the spokeswoman for common sense and fair play, she knows well enough not to stifle the semi-hysterical energy of her horse-crazy daughter, and she lets the girl have her dream.

Audiences and critics loved Liz. "Her face is alive with youthful spirit," wrote Bosley Crowther in *The New York Times*, "her voice has the softness of sweet song and her whole manner . . . is one of refreshing grace." In the years to come, critics were not always so enchanted.

Taylor grew up too quickly,

THE WHITE CLIFFS OF DOVER (1944). With Roddy McDowall

and her tenure as child star was brief. Velvet Brown, in fact, is her only major child star role. Sandwiched between Lassie and the horse story are tiny parts in *Jane Eyre* (1944) [on loan-out to Fox] and *The White Cliffs of Dover* (1944). In the former, she's a saint, the comforter of young Jane at Lowood, the Dick-

ensian home for orphaned children. In the latter, as a little girl who woos the heroine's son, she's a child version of the Taylor ingenue. As a tender and delicate child in *Jane Eyre*, she breaks the rules in order to share some of her food with her friend who's been confined to solitary. Young Elizabeth is used to represent the spirit of charity and goodness, cautioning Jane that she mustn't speak wickedly about others, no matter what they may have done to her. Even here, though, as a vision of childlike purity, there are almost unconscious suggestions of the siren-to-be—her flowing hair antagonizes the prim headmaster. After being locked out in the rain, the frail, other-worldly little Helen dies, with Jane clasped in her arms.

It's a lovely cameo, sentimental without being sticky: a radiant child as saint on earth.

After *National Velvet*, MGM had only one project for its new star, a programmer called *The Courage of Lassie* (1946). The dog gets top billing, but Liz has plenty of crying and hugging to do as a supremely devoted mistress. Another homespun saga, filmed in the spectacular Northwest, the film (which

JANE EYRE (1944). With Eily Malyon, Henry Daniell, and Peggy Ann Garner

COURAGE OF LASSIE (1946). With Lassie and Frank Morgan

begins with a long, curious, wild-life sequence) mixes farm family folksiness with an odd dog story: Lassie goes to a training school for war dogs, is shipped to the front and performs heroically. Returned to America, the dog suffers a nervous collapse, becoming a menace to society. In the last reel, though, corrected and tamed by her loving owner, Lassie is not only exonerated, she's proclaimed a war hero.

The movie is thus the story of the shell-shocked, maladjusted veteran as a dog. The conceit is absurd, of course, and reviewers objected to the exploitation of a serious subject. But as the willful farm girl who finds a dog, loses a

COURAGE OF LASSIE (1946). With Lassie

dog, and regains a dog, Liz is again the overwrought, ecstatic child, lavishing her attention on Lassie. As Agee noted, she can turn on various speeds of frenzied excitement in a second. Her big moments are a tearful courtroom scene, in which she pleads with the judge to give her back her dog, and the last scene when, as Lassie returns, she collapses in a torrent of joyous tears.

Because her greatest fame came later, as a young woman, most people forget what a skillful child actress she was. Less burdened than at any later time by her beauty and fame, she is at her least self-conscious in these early performances. Untouched, she reveals in these animal stories her natural flair for tears and hugs—the paraphernalia of an emotional female.

After *The Courage of Lassie*, when she was entering an awkward transitional period from child to teen-ager—a period that few child performers have been able to bridge—MGM wisely kept her under wraps. She studied at the studio school, and the publicity department devised a series of gimmicks to keep her name before the public: the studio gave her the horse she rode to victory in *National Velvet*; she wrote a book, *Nibbles and Me*, about her pet chipmunk; she sold a painting; and, on her fourteenth birthday, she was given her own car. Off-screen, but still in public view, Elizabeth Taylor matured from spiritual child to curvy teen-ager. By fifteen, she was prepared to launch her career as a silver screen *femme fatale*.

She came back (though she'd never really been away) with a Taylor-made vehicle: in *Cynthia* (1947), not a horse, not a dog, but Elizabeth Taylor, is the star. Directed competently by Robert Z. Leonard, it's a minor movie that hardly anybody remembers, but it provides a nice cushion between animals and boys, between the pre-erotic and the full-fledged romantic Liz.

Based on a foolish play, *The Rich Full Life*, by a resolutely

PUPPY LOVE

old-fashioned playwright named Viña Delmar, *Cynthia* is the story of a girl tyrannized by parents who think she's too delicate for the likes of this world. Kept in a protected, glass menagerie kind of environment, pampered and petted, Cynthia hasn't been allowed to grow up in a normal way. But with the help of a mother (Mary Astor) who's willing to bend, and a music teacher (S. Z. Sakall) who thinks she's a princess, Cynthia makes it to the prom—and survives.

As in *Jane Eyre*, Taylor is cast as an ethereal beauty. The part bears no resemblance to Elizabeth Taylor in her latest shrew phase, but it does effectively exploit her early image as a young girl set apart from other kids. The role of lonely Cynthia complemented the Taylor publicity of the time: because she was a famous movie actress, young Liz was isolated from others her own age. Other teen-agers were either afraid or jealous of her, and if you believe the *Photoplay* gossip of the time, Elizabeth had trouble getting a date.

CYNTHIA (1947). With S. Z. Sakall

The character of Cynthia taps the sweet, innocent side of Liz. With her precise diction and her obedient manner, she has something of the carriage of the best behaved little girl in the class, but her performance has a kind of grave charm. The movie's slogan was "Her First Kiss!" but Taylor's romance with Jimmy Lydon (who was also her heartthrob in *Life With Father*) is decidedly pre-erotic:

she's sweet rather than sexy in this one.

Like many of the early Taylor movies, *Cynthia* has the candy-coated flavor of a Booth Tarkington novel ("a synthetic morsel—right out of the Metro candy box," snipped Bosley Crowther). The movie is homespun Americana, complete with fireside chats with Mummy and clear distinctions between the snooty rich relatives and the poor decent folks. (*Cynthia* is one of the few times in her career in which Taylor played one of the latter.)

The last scene, in which Liz bounds into the living room, confounding her parents' fear that going to the prom on a rainy night would do her in, is her declaration of independence: bright and energetic, all set to become part of a normal teen-age life, Cynthia (and movie star Liz) are now all grown-up and ready for action.

In *A Date with Judy* (1948), another slice of teen-age life as seen from the back lot at Culver City, Liz is fully absorbed in the world of men that is to preoccupy her for the rest of her career. This time, she's the poor little rich girl, snooty and out for trouble because she has a father problem: like many of her menfolk to come, Daddy's real attention is elsewhere, on making money.

Unhappy at home, she stirs up trouble abroad, giving naive Jane Powell bad advice on how to handle boys, and stealing one of Jane's boyfriends right out from under her twitching nose.

CYNTHIA (1947). With Mary Astor and George Murphy

A DATE WITH JUDY (1948). With Jane Powell

Very pre-Lolita, a Forties style teen-aged sex kitten, this is the first version of the Taylor minx and she seems highly sophisticated for a small-town high school girl, even if she *is* rich.

A thoroughly good-natured musical, antiseptic and cheery, deliberately cornball and aimed at none too bright teen-agers, *A Date with Judy* is vintage MGM: it suggests Hollywood's conception of high school life in the Forties. *The New York Times* called the movie "acceptable summer entertainment" that "follows the apparently immutable cinematic rule that all American adolescents are basically noble in their intentions but are handicapped by idiocy."

Like *Cynthia*, the film is very class conscious, contrasting Taylor's cold, upper class household with Jane Powell's comfortable, but decidedly lower-notched, middle-class home. Typically, Liz is rich, spoiled, and aloof, but typically, too, when all is said and done, she's no brat; she's a good kid who just needs a little love and attention. At the end, she's made up with best friend Judy, with her father, and with Robert Stack, the guy she wins.

She wasn't the star, but Taylor received excellent notices. She had more presence than anyone else in the movie, and the part finally allowed her to use the sexiness that everyone had sensed since she rode that horse in *National Velvet*. Otis Guernsey, in the *New York Herald Tribune*, wrote that "the erstwhile

A DATE WITH JUDY (1948). With Leon Ames

LIFE WITH FATHER (1947). With William Powell and ZaSu Pitts

star of *National Velvet* . . . has been touched by Metro's magic wand and turned into a real, fourteen-carat, one-hundred-proof siren with a whole new career opening in front of her." Liz was an audience favorite too; from June to November, she received 1,065 bids to college proms.

Liz had no leading roles from *Cynthia* in 1947 to *Conspir-*

ator in 1950, but MGM used her sensibly, casting her in parts that allowed her to grow up at a plausible speed. In *Life With Father* (1947), made on loan-out to Warners, she's another queen of puppy love. A visiting country cousin impressed by the big city, she flirts with the eldest Day boy, making eyes, demanding attention, standing on amorous ceremonies, all in the best *jeune* cocotte Taylor manner. Pert and sassy, easily provoked to tears, she's a real charmer in this film, but even here she has trouble with the men: Clarence isn't quite demonstrative enough for her, and he doesn't promise to be the *first* one to write. (After all, the proper young girl reasons, it's the man who must write first, declaring his undying love.)

By 1948, she was ready for grown-up romance, and in *Julia Misbehaves*, she receives her first *serious* screen kiss from Peter Lawford. Her love scenes, in fact, convinced MGM that their mature sixteen-year-old was prepared to take on adult roles. But Taylor's romancing is secondary, the film being designed as a showcase for Greer Garson to prove that Metro's gracious tea-serving lady had some fun in her. As the misbehaving Julia, a circus trouper and woman about town, Garson cuts up in a misguided effort to erase the fact that she ever played Mrs. Miniver. In *The New York*

JULIA MISBEHAVES (1948). With Greer Garson and Peter Lawford

LITTLE WOMEN (1949). With Margaret O'Brien, Janet Leigh, and June Allyson

Times, Bosley Crowther called the movie "a fantastic knocka-bout farce which discovers Miss Garson in a bathtub and leaves her in a puddle of mud."

Taylor plays the decorative ingenue, saved at the end from marrying the wrong man. She merely had to look pretty, and

it's the first time that she seems like a slick made-up movie starlet and nothing else.

But in her next film, *Little Women* (1949), she was given a chance to play comedy, and as the selfish, flighty Amy who loves to eat and who misuses big words (she calls their old neighbor "perfectionary"), she's a delight. Critics and audiences were preoccupied with the inferiority of the Mervyn LeRoy version to the 1936 George Cukor film, but the later rendition has one advantage over its illustrious predecessor: as Amy, the trivial and dizzy vixen and the most engaging of the tear-stained March sisters, Liz has much more spirit than Joan Bennett.

Despite her evident flair for the barbed line and the witty retort, MGM didn't use her for comedy. Preoccupied to the point of distraction over affairs of the heart, she was the reigning young tragic actress in the early Fifties, cast in a series of soulful parts. Her Amy, therefore, is a charming respite, a light-hearted version of the women in love who were the staple of her upcoming ingenue period.

Sparked by Liz in an uncharacteristic daffy part and unfolding before us as a series of lushly tinted papier-maché picture postcards, this second *Little Women* is perfectly respectable. It has the requisite portions of giddy comedy and soap opera heart tug; Margaret O'Brien suffers nobly, Janet Leigh smiles sweetly, June Allyson tries valiantly, and what more could be asked of Louisa May Alcott's perfumed perennial?

Little Women marked an end to Taylor's child-woman phase. Part giggly teen-ager, a flighty girl who looks at life from the angle of a Victorian romance, part incipient flirt, coyly but kindly stealing Laurie away from older sister Jo, her Amy is a pleasing mixture of the Taylor innocent and the Taylor minx.

In 1950, in a movie publicized as her first adult role, Liz, for the first time since *Cynthia*, was queen of her own harem. *Conspirator* was designed to guide Taylor from young girl to woman in much the same way that *Cynthia* moved her from child to young girl. As the movie opens, she's an American deb in London, worrying over being asked for a dance at a ball, and preoccupied with shopping sprees. Like many of the parts she's played, her young lady here is a person with nothing on her mind. Scatter-brained, superficial, devil-may-care, Liz is yet a beguiling flirt; there's a particularly charming scene early in the film in which she chatters foolishly and at length in order to allay her fears of the dark.

The business of the movie is to take her from giddy deb to bruised but knowing young woman, and the change is effected, of course, by her relations with a man. After a whirlwind courtship, she marries a handsome older man, a soldier who's the answer to her schoolgirl notions of romance. With typical Taylor luck, her husband turns out to be a spy for the Russians. When she finally discovers his double life, she decides to turn him in. Her scene of momentous moral decision is unique in the

THE WRONG MAN

Taylor canon: it's the only time in her career that romance is mixed with politics.

In its own simplistic way, *Conspirator* is a message movie, and Taylor, for a change, is the *raisonneuse*, expressing dismay at her husband's duplicity and urging him to the greater rewards of loyalty to country. Liz is a patriot; as she says, she doesn't know much about politics, but, instinctively, she knows right from wrong and what her husband is doing is wrong.

A vehicle for "aging" Liz, *Conspirator* is also, of course, Hollywood's response to the early Fifties Communist scare. The film is a firm warning that Communist sympathizers will end unhappily. (The husband— Robert Taylor—kills himself, torn fatally between love and duty.) In 1950, Hollywood couldn't possibly conceive of a *human* Communist, and so they cast an automaton in a robot role: Taylor is a remarkably dull actor. As storm warning or political statement, *Conspirator* is Fifties naive; as a vehicle for Taylor's transition from girl to

CONSPIRATOR (1950) As
Melinda Greyton

CONSPIRATOR (1950)
With Robert Taylor

woman, it has a modest appeal.

Conspirator, though, marks the beginning of Taylor's blandest phase. From 1950 to 1954, as she was entering the ripest period of her young womanhood, MGM finally opened the flood gates for her, exploiting the prettiest girl in the studio in a way they hadn't in the Forties. A full-fledged ingenue by this time, Taylor appeared in twelve films in a five-year period, moving without much discrimination from programmers to prestige packages. *Conspirator* and *The Big Hangover* were cheek-by-jowl with *A Place in the Sun*; low-budget fudge like *Love is Better Than Ever* followed classy kitsch like *Father of the Bride*.

In most of these, Taylor was the airy representative of the American rich, the Daddy's Girl who had everything. Never getting exactly what she wanted, though, she was seldom happy. In her two archetypal roles of the period, the American princess in George Stevens' *A Place in the Sun* (1951) and the high-living expatriate in *The Last Time I Saw Paris* (1954), she loses her man in the one and her life in the other. Rich and envied, protected and privileged, she is yet a vulnerable, unfulfilled woman.

There are in these middle-period movies signs and tokens of the sharp-tongued defensive shrew that would follow a decade later, but in all these movies she's movie-star charming, a well-trained young lady, a deb on the verge of entering the junior league and its regimen of charities and gala balls. In the Fifties, Taylor glides like a swan through a world of silver coffee service and discreet servants, lawn parties and weekends in the country.

The meaty Taylor parts, in the Stevens film and in *The Last Time I Saw Paris*, were commonly regarded as her first real acting jobs. Variety suggested that her "histrionics" in *A Place in the Sun* "are of a quality so far beyond anything she had done previously that Stevens' skilled hands on the reins must be credited with a minor miracle." But no one who had seen *Little Women* or *A Date with Judy* or, for that matter, *National Velvet* or *Courage of Lassie*, could possibly insist that Stevens' movie contained her first "acting" performance.

Reversing Victorian stereotype, she plays the good dark heroine to Shelley Winters' bad blonde heroine; she's the spirit of beauty and romance to Winters' oppressed and nagging working girl. In her finest moment, she describes, in a hushed, breathy

A PLACE IN THE SUN (1951). With Montgomery Clift and Shepperd Strudwick

voice, the beauty of the lake and the surrounding countryside as they appear in the early morning mist; Stevens tapped a sensitivity that hadn't been used since *Jane Eyre,* and in this scene Taylor's beauty comes from within.

The movie adaptation of Theodore Dreiser's heavyweight *An American Tragedy* is, of course, a reduction of the book: consider the change in title. The movie softens the sharp social indictment of the original; as the film presents them, the events of George Eastman's history could never support Dreiser's grandiose title. This is a movie about a decent man locked in the ancient conflict between love and honor.

A PLACE IN THE SUN (1951). With Montgomery Clift

Drawn to the world of the very rich, which comes tantalizingly within reach, he is held back, stifled, by the claims of poverty. His story, as told here, is more a romantic triangle than an American Tragedy.

In fact, *A Place in the Sun* is one of the best of the Taylor triangle movies. Montgomery Clift, the man in the middle, is dazzled by Liz and pursued by Shelley Winters. Winters had the showier role, but Taylor was surprisingly effective as what she was supposed to be, the girl of every man's dreams.

The other prestige film Tay-

THE LAST TIME I SAW PARIS (1954). With Roger Moore and Van Johnson

lor made during this period was not as successful. An expansion of "Babylon Revisited," the swift, trenchant F. Scott Fitzgerald short story, *The Last Time I Saw Paris* converts the author's sensibility downward, to pathos and soap opera. "The soft soap is smeared so smoothly," wrote Bosley Crowther in the *Times*, "and that old Jerome Kern tune is played so insistently that it may turn the public's heart to toothpaste." The movie thus betrays the dry-eyed spirit of the original material. The first mistake, though, was in changing the era from the Lost Generation Twenties to post-World War II. The jazz age ambiance, recollected in the story, the mystique of Paris in the Twenties—these key tokens of Fitzgerald's sensibility are missing.

Even more damaging than the switch in era is the attempt to expand the characters whose motivations are only sketched lightly in the short story. Van Johnson is clearly playing a variant on the fabled author himself, and Elizabeth Taylor suggests a watered-down version of Zelda. The script borrows from the legend of Scotty and Zelda, the desperate, high-living couple whirling madly through a sophisticated Old World city. But their fatal contamination of each other —his bent of self-destructiveness, her inertia and instability—is barely approached. A complex, mythic mismatch is treated with ladies' magazine gloss. The movie and the actors do not move the characters from point A to point B: why, for instance, do husband and wife reverse roles, she transformed from party girl to sober wife who wants to go home to America, he collapsing from earnest writer to disappointed drunk, the Great American Novel maddeningly eluding him?

The characters change (she rises, he plummets) because that's what it says in the script. Van Johnson lacks the mythic stature or the coiled depths to suggest other than a poor man's version of the great, doomed Fitzgerald. And Liz was too young and untried at the time to embody an arch-neurotic, part wicked temptress, and part ministering angel.

The role is a summation of the Taylor ingenue: the good-time flirt, cunningly stealing a man from her older sister; the spoiled daughter of a fast living phony; the irresponsible party girl with a good heart underneath it all; the sober young mother and wife; the defiant adulteress; the frail spirit felled by the forces of nature (a night

THE LAST TIME I SAW PARIS (1954). With Van Johnson

in the Paris damp gives her a fatal case of pneumonia). At each "station," she is on home ground, but the part comes out in bits and pieces rather than a coherent whole: the character, finally, does not add up. It may be partly Taylor vapidity (Beverly Hills didn't prepare her for Paris), but it's also the script and the direction: that saintly woman, dying of pneumonia and forgiving all, has very little connection to the blithe spirit who steals her sister's man and parties with non-stop frenzy.

The other ingenue roles in the period from *Conspirator* to *The Last Time I Saw Paris* are less challenging, but almost all are pleasing. The best of them are the two joyous Vincente Minnelli comedies, *Father of the Bride* (1950) and *Father's Little Dividend* (1951). Like many Taylor films, they are endearing specimens of Hollywood Americana.

A minor classic in a minor tradition, blending the late Forties with the early Fifties, *Father of the Bride* is a pre-*Father Knows Best* peek at a distressingly average upper-middle-class family. The Bankses are your typical consumer-oriented suburbanites who follow the rules. Robert Hatch, in *The New Republic*, suggested that they represent "the perfect flowering of the American dream. . . . They live in modest luxury according to the best mortgage-plan principles. They are people who ride in Dynaflow, cruise in the West Indies, demand high fidelity, exclaim at the wholesome goodness of sealed-in freshness, display a weekly wash that is the envy of the neighborhood."[°]

One night at dinner, daughter Kay casually announces her engagement. Like the situation comedy parents they are, father and mother react on cue. Ozzie and Harriet of the Big Screen, Mr. and Mrs. Banks fret and fume their way right up to the day of reckoning. Following practically to the letter the events of Edward Streeter's charming, light-as-a-feather novel, the movie is a series of comic set pieces: father meets future son-in-law; boy's parents meet girl's parents; prospective bride feuds with prospective groom. The vignettes are brushed with the light Minnelli touch at its most beguiling, and they are acted with captivating nonchalance by Spencer Tracy, Joan Bennett, and the Taylors, Don and Elizabeth.

As the put-upon, grumbling

°Robert Hatch, *The New Republic*, June 12, 1950.

FATHER OF THE BRIDE (1950). With Don Taylor

FATHER OF THE BRIDE (1950). With Spencer Tracy

FATHER'S LITTLE DIVIDEND (1951). with Spencer Tracy, Don Taylor, Moroni Olsen, Billie Burke, and Joan Bennett

teddy bear papa, solicitous of his daughter's welfare and vigilant as to the disposal of his pennies, Tracy is unbeatably droll. Playing the American domestic dictator (a role in the tradition of Clarence Day in *Life with Father*), Tracy is all good-natured bluff and he-man heartiness. But it's an ensemble show, and as the typical spoiled daughter of a typical mid-American bourgeois, Elizabeth has one of her happiest

screen moments, twisting and cajoling her father and her fiance with a guile instinctive to the natural-born female. Except for her blithe announcement of her engagement, when she chatters mindlessly about her fiance's prospects and The Life Ahead, she has no scene all for herself. She's there to supply the steady background hum, and this is one of her most responsive and natural performances. Like the film

THE GIRL WHO HAD EVERYTHING (1953). With William Powell

itself, she's as light as air.

Detailing the life of the newlyweds (does he really love her?) and the traumas attendant upon the birth of the first baby, *Father's Little Dividend* is more of the same, a movie as cozy and as dependent on little shocks of recognition as its predecessor. Guided with the Minnelli grace, the movie is that rare thing—a sequel that retains the freshness of the original.

These two movies are some-thing of a curiosity in Taylor's career. It wasn't too often that Liz got the chance to play a completely average young lady, the charming girl next door rather than the rich and unattainable beauty. In *Cynthia* or *A Date with Judy*, she's someone set apart from the prom crowd. Here, as bride-to-be or as eager, fretful wife and mother, she's a healthy, normal young woman, something of a forerunner to Elinor Donohue's bright, bubbly

THE GIRL WHO HAD EVERYTHING (1953). With Fernando Lamas

Betty of *Father Knows Best*.

In her high ingenue phase, Liz made her four most undistinguished movies. *Conspirator* and *The Big Hangover* in 1950, *Love is Better Than Ever* in 1952, and *The Girl Who Had Everything* in 1953, are decidedly lower case entries. She was a star at the time, and considering the care Metro gave her in the Forties, her appearance in these programmers is surprising. They are all the kind of second feature black-and-white quickies that are now the province of the Made for Television factories. But these four self-effacing movies are showcases for Liz in a way that most of her earlier films had not been: except for *The Big Hangover*, she's at the center of the movies.

In three of these, she's in her usual rich world milieu. In *The Big Hangover*, she's the boss's daughter; in *Conspirator*, she's an American debutante in London; in *The Girl Who Had Everything*, she's the daughter of a big-time lawyer. In *Love is Better Than Ever*, she has one of her few working girl roles; a small-town dancing teacher who comes to the big city for a convention and falls for a smart-talking theatrical agent.

In these four items (and in the somewhat more elevated *Elephant Walk*), Taylor is cast as the innocent who chooses the wrong guy. She's the hapless partner in a classic mismatch. In both *Love is Better Than Ever* and *The Girl Who Had Everything* (the titles tell all), she's a spirited young lady with a mind of her own. In the former, she defies her small-town upbringing by coyly tempting the fates as she romances a city slicker. In the latter, she challenges her father in order to run off with a *bon vivant* with underworld associations. In *Conspirator*, the wretched girl marries a Communist. In *The Big Hangover*, she's engaged to a man with a drinking problem. And in *Elephant Walk*, her husband is a madman with a father fixation.

These five ladies are variations on the young Taylor woman, an innocent who thinks she knows more than she does. In each movie, she has to be educated; the reckless spirit has to be confined and corrected. At the end of *The Girl Who Had Everything* after her unhappy fling with a man not of her class or her character, rich father William Powell lectures her on the virtues of home and the family. Liz listens carefully to his speech on the contentments of the quiet domestic life, and she leaves the big city in order to re-

LOVE IS BETTER THAN EVER (1952). With Larry Parks

turn home to the Virginia countryside; presumably, now that her feathers have been trimmed, she will marry an eligible and *safe* young man.

Love is Better Than Ever offers the same town-country split. This time, Liz is even more provincial, an innocent tempted but never corrupted by big city dissipation. A pixie who falls for a slangy Broadway agent (Larry Parks), Liz is once again the determined pursuer, setting her sights on a man who does not want to marry. Impudent and headstrong, a vixen spreading her net, she decides to announce her engagement, hoping (like Maggie the Cat five years later) that fiction may stimulate fact.

In *Elephant Walk*, the cultural difference between the heroine and her man is much more exotic. Taylor is a dreamy London shopgirl whisked off to be the mistress of a Ceylonese plantation. But again, the man she marries has a problem. (With Taylor, a basically sane sort herself, it's almost always the man who's maladjusted.) Her husband (Peter Finch) is obsessed by the memory of his autocratic father, and it's the dead father whose spirit runs the plantation. What with trying to fight a dead man, ridding the plantation of her husband's drinking companions, locking horns with a

ELEPHANT WALK (1954). With Dana Andrews

ELEPHANT WALK (1954). As Ruth Wiley, caught in an elephant stampede

THE BIG HANGOVER (1950). With Van Johnson

high-minded major domo, coping with a cholera epidemic, and getting no love at home, Taylor certainly has her hands full. Overwrought and rebuffed, she gratefully accepts the kindly attentions of her husband's overseer (Dana Andrews).

It's another Taylor triangle picture, and something of a dry run for her role as the visiting wife in *Giant*. A mini-epic, beefed up with exotic locales, a climatic elephant stampede and native rites, *Elephant Walk* is, in fact, something of a poor man's *Giant*. A pot-boiler for a lazy Saturday, the movie gave Liz a change of scenery, and allowed her more spunk and self-respect than most of her other willful debutante-rebels. The wife here has a sharp tongue and a strong will, and so there are intimations of the spitfire to come. Stepping in after Vivien Leigh became too ill to complete the role, Taylor plays her movie star, ladies' fiction heroine with more spirit than she was given credit for.

The Big Hangover is the only film of this period in which the Taylor ingenue is peripheral. "Dressed up like a mannequin," wrote Otis Guernsey in the *Herald Tribune*, "she has merely to appear interested or affectionate." Under its romantic comedy fluff about the boss's daughter and the army veteran for whom a whiff of brandy means instant inebriation, the movie is a message picture—about discrimination in housing, of all things. But Liz, Hollywood's idle woman, has no part in the movie's more sober passages: the world's work, and the film's moral center, go on without her. Van Johnson, as a noble lawyer who defends minorities, has the heroic decisions; Liz stays at home, and it's almost as if her allure interferes with the man's important work.

The subsidiary theme of Liz as interference is barely hinted at within the split personality of *The Big Hangover*. But it's the main theme of *Rhapsody*, her 1954 star vehicle that unconsciously sabotages her at the same time that it's constructed as an homage to her beauty.

Another pampered lady of wealth, another rebellious daughter of another rich man, Liz is the destructive element in the lives of two musicians. A girl with a lot of time on her hands, she craves attention. So, while Vittorio Gassman intently practices his scales, the poor little rich girl tickles his ears or reclines languidly on elegantly upholstered divans. The lady's not bad, you understand, or mean—she's just a drain because she doesn't *do* anything but ask to be loved. She's the aimless *femme fatale*, the idle jet set flirt: decorative, but useless.

As usual, Taylor plays a woman who can't, and doesn't have to, do anything. It's the men who are the geniuses. Gassman, a tough-minded sort, will not mix business with pleasure; for this stick-in-the-mud, the fiddle comes first—its art before Liz. But John Ericson, a brilliant pianist, cannot so easily resist the Taylor enchantment, and he knuckles under, taking to drink under the strain of living with Liz and her millions.

Metro always allowed Taylor to redeem herself. She's the

RHAPSODY (1954). With Vittorio Gassman

naughty girl gone *temporarily* rather than permanently astray: she stays around long enough to rehabilitate her collapsed genius, restoring him to a place of honor in the musical world and establishing her own credentials as a decent person after all.

A woman who has only her beauty to recommend her, whose unemployable beauty is in fact a threat to art—movie myths are not made of parts like this. The role's conception is anti-star. Taking their cue from the film itself, reviewers gushed over the star's appearance; mesmerized by her looks, they were mum as to her acting. *Newsweek* wrote that Taylor "swoons beautifully to the airs of Peter Ilyitch Tchaikovsky and Sergei Rachmaninoff . . . in a woman's picture de luxe." Less charitably, Otis Guernsey in the *Herald Tribune* suggested that "the point

RHAPSODY (1954). With John Ericson

IVANHOE (1952). With Robert Taylor

of the whole story is to show off Elizabeth Taylor wearing attractive gowns, sobbing in loneliness, or radiant at a concert . . . it looks as though Miss Taylor's charm had struck every one senseless, leaving nothing but this charm for the movie to go on."

But even as a vacant American princess abroad or as a useless ingenue on the sidelines in a no-account romantic comedy, Taylor is more at home than in medieval or Regency England. As the people who later produced *Cleopatra* should have realized, Taylor's a modern; she hasn't the voice or the imagination to play a lady from another time. In *Ivanhoe*, impersonating Rebecca, the Jewess accused of sorcery, the competitor of fair Saxon Lady Rowena for the hand of Ivanhoe (miraculously, Rebecca loses), Liz is stately but inescapably contemporary. About to go to the stake, she pouts and simpers like a girl stood up for a heavy Saturday night date.

The movie is kitsch in which hints of personal drama (and pleas for religious tolerance) periodically interrupt the procession of jousts and tournaments and hand to hand combats. The Tay-

IVANHOE (1952). Rebecca at the stake.

IVANHOE (1952). With George Sanders

BEAU BRUMMEL (1954). With James Donald

lors, Robert and Elizabeth, and Joan Fontaine, are stiff and dignified and vacuous, but then the Sir Walter Scott originals are hardly compelling.

For Rebecca, Liz sports her little-girl-on-her-best-behavior composure (she's sweet, she tries), but in *Beau Brummel* (1954), she's downright silly. The voice will not do for a highly placed Regency maiden. With its lavish appointments and its scene-stealing histrionics from Peter Ustinov and Robert Morley as the dotty Prince of Wales and his even dottier father King George III, the movie is not as bad as you might expect. The rooms look authentic, and, when

BEAU BRUMMEL (1954). With Stewart Granger

Ustinov is jabbering away delightfully as the petty, vain, trendy monarch to be, the film even sounds authentic. But the illusion is destroyed whenever Taylor speaks in the unmistakable accent and pitch of Wilshire Boulevard.

As Lady Patricia, Taylor is tossed on a sea of romantic indecision. She must choose between the impetuous adventurer and a sober court politician. A little bourgeoise at heart, she opts finally for the harbor rather than the tempest.

Richard Mansfield, the American stage actor whose specialty was stentorian heroes in the romantic tradition, commissioned Clyde Fitch to write the history of the Regency's pre-eminent man of mode as a vehicle for his talents. The movie is based on Fitch's play, but with a pallid Stewart Granger as the notorious fashion-monger, the focus is wisely shifted to the wacky Regent. Ustinov's Regent has more glamor than Granger's pale soldier of fortune, and the movie becomes the story of the misguided, easily manipulated, finally rather pathetic Prince of Wales rather than a showcase for the era's swaggering and theatrical beau.

As a character study of fashion-crazed royalty, *Beau Brummel* is entertaining fustian; as romance, or as insight into the historical Beau himself, the movie is impoverished. Granger and his leading lady are responsible for the dead weight that surrounds Ustinov's spirited, Oscar Wilde-like tomfoolery.

The rich, willful Taylor in-genues contained intimations of the Southern belles to follow, but even at her ripest, in *A Place in the Sun* or *The Last Time I Saw Paris*, Liz had not fully awak-ened to the best that was in her. *Giant* turned the trick, and from the George Stevens epic in 1956 to *Butterfield 8* in 1960—her major phase—Taylor broke out of the pleasant ingenue mold to become a full-fledged actress. The range was never dazzling, but the talent was genuine.

The archetypal Taylor of this high period was, of course, the Southern belle, saucy, coy, quick-tempered, nailing down her men with her practiced femi-nine wiles and her smoldering, beckoning sexiness. The parts were nothing she hadn't done before, but, rising to the chal-lenge of much heftier material than her usual MGM pastry, Taylor performed vividly. The ingenue who glided gracefully and almost always competently through studio fluff proved she had personality, intensity, and humor.

In *Raintree County*, the Taylor belle goes mad. In *Sud-denly, Last Summer* she's fight-ing to hold on to her sanity. In *Giant* and *Cat on a Hot Tin Roof*, the lady is steady as the Rock of Gibraltar. But whether

THE CAT

flighty or sober, collapsible or steadfast, the heroines are all ab-solutely determined: the girls in *Raintree County* and *Cat on a Hot Tin Roof* want their man, and they'll deceive and claw and play dirty to get him; the wife in *Giant* wants to be herself rather than the way Texas ladies of her station are supposed to be; the bewildered girl in *Suddenly, Last Summer* just wants to keep her mind.

Fighters all, these ladies are rebels of a sort, doing what they want to do even if that means challenging the Southern code. Four stubborn women: four love-ly performances that comprise the highest and most sustained creative streak in Taylor's career.

Giant elevated Elizabeth Taylor to superstardom. After it, there were no more program-mers. Until *Cleopatra*, the agen-da was one prestige film a year, for all of which she received Oscar nominations.

A high Fifties epic, three and a half hours of gorgeous commercial celluloid, *Giant* met the lush, sprawling Edna Ferber novel on its own level. Detailing

GIANT (1956). With Rock Hudson

the history of a Texas royal family, the movie, like the novel, is a monument to myths about Texas size, wealth, and vulgarity. A well-bred lady from Virginia, Liz is the outsider who marries the burly, thick-headed ruler of a family dynasty (Rock Hudson) and who stubbornly refuses to forfeit her own notions of right and wrong. In choosing as his bride this independent woman who won't conform to Texas folkways, Bick Benedict selected a wily and persevering antagonist, a lady with a mind of her own who challenges, and loves, him every step of the way. At the end, when he fights the owner of a roadside diner who will not serve his Mexican daughter-in-law and grandchild, Liz can count the twenty-five-year battle hers. Playing the liberal to her husband's reactionary, she's succeeded finally in educating her man. (It's one of the few occasions when Taylor's the wise

GIANT (1956). With James Dean

GIANT (1956). With James Dean

teacher rather than the recalcitrant pupil.)

The marriage—a prototype for the Taylor ménage, in which tenderness and turbulence are closely mingled—is set against the evolution of Texas from old-fashioned to modern. As horse-loving Virginia deb, as new bride, as threat to her husband's mannish domineering sister, as young wife and mother, as patrona of the ranch who would rather talk politics with the men than chit-chat with the women, as the unattainable mistress of Jett Rink's dreams, as dignified, middle-aged champion of American-Chicano integration, Liz is at the center of the epic canvas, and it's a wise and charming performance. Stevens again taps the stillness of her serene beauty, but he also explores the temperament of the Taylor spitfire. Luz Benedict is one of Taylor's strong heroines, one of the few women she's played who, if they abso-

RAINTREE COUNTY (1957). As Susanna Drake

lutely had to, might make it on their own.

In *Giant*, Liz was the conventional, though tough-minded, heroine of ladies' magazine fiction. In *Raintree County*, as a disturbed Louisiana lady with a fixation that she's part black, she has a character part. She's the heavy, the raven-haired poisonous *femme fatale* to Eva Marie Saint's inevitable lily-livered heroine. As in *A Place in the Sun*, Liz is used as the symbol of a particular social class and a particular kind of woman: as Philip Roth wrote in *The New Republic*, she represents "the sensualist-aristocrat in whose world elegance and indulgence are hardly distinguishable." The dark lady of the sonnets, the wicked temptress, she sets her mark on an idealistic young man (Montgomery Clift) who's looking for the golden tree that contains the secret of the meaning of life. Trapping him into marriage with the lie that she's pregnant, and then proceeding to lose her hold on her sanity, the Taylor vamp detains a good and helpless man for eight years. He is released, able to return to his magnificent dreams and to his pure childhood sweetheart, only after her death.

Retaining the thrust of the mammoth Ross Lockridge, Jr., novel, the movie equates the unhappy romance with the Civil War: the personal drama is thus a reflection of the nation's wounds. According to the topheavy symbolism, Taylor represents the South, polluting and

RAINTREE COUNTY (1957). With Montgomery Clift

CAT ON A HOT TIN ROOF (1958). With Paul Newman

dragging down the North; she's the Body contaminating the poet's Soul. At the end of the Civil War, Susanna Drake takes her life, and the poet, like the country, is cleansed.

Divested of her strenuous symbolic function, the character is one of the showiest Taylor ever played. For the only time in her career, Taylor is a loony. When we first meet her, the most troubled of the Taylor belles is all flounce and giggles, all coy Southern charm, but she's a vampire at heart, draining the life from her husband. Susanna isn't hateful, but she's certainly not good for Johnny Shawnessy, and she's a nuisance to herself as well.

The character's tortured family background is gaudy bestseller melodrama, but Taylor plays it at full volume, with a flair and an intensity that surpass all her earlier work. In her big confession scene, wide-eyed with recollected horror, she tells her poor husband of the demons that haunt her: her fear of black blood, and her memory of the traumatic night that her crazed mother, suspecting her husband of sleeping with a mulatto servant, set fire to the white-pillared family mansion.

MGM tried to market *Raintree County* as another *Gone With the Wind*, which it isn't. For all its fierce symbol-mongering and its compulsively florid writing, Lockridge's thousand-page examination of the American character isn't the great bad novel that Margaret Mitchell's perennial is. But with its battles and its formal balls, its palatial riverboats and decayed mansions, its bordellos and madhouses, its childbirth and deathbed scenes, and its evacuation of Atlanta, the movie, like its source, has undeniable epic sweep. Montgomery Clift as the hapless poet and Eva Marie Saint as his childhood sweetheart and true love are on the sticky side, but the scenes with Liz strike fire in a wonderfully hokey way. An overripe and quite mad Southern woman who contains presentiments of the later *Virginia Woolf* shrew, Susanna Drake is among Taylor's most colorful and complete characterizations.

The two Tennessee Williams films that followed are the high-water mark of her career. In

CAT ON A HOT TIN ROOF (1958).
With Paul Newman.

83

CAT ON A HOT TIN ROOF (1958). As Maggie

Cat on a Hot Tin Roof (1958) and *Suddenly, Last Summer* (1959) she channels her new-found energy into *bona fide* literary commodities rather than slick, bestselling epics. The two plays are among Williams' most sustained and urgent performances as well. Intensely theatrical, sparked by sardonic dialogue, the plays are great box-office melodramas. And with their literary flourishes and their coiled characterizations, they are the best material Taylor ever had to work with. She goes at her roles with the restless, lunging thrusts of a prize race horse at the starting gate.

The Pollitts, the eccentric family in *Cat on a Hot Tin Roof*, squabble bitchily for two hours over who will inherit Big Daddy's 28,000 acres of "the richest land this side of the Valley Nile." The real center of the drama, though, is not the battle for possession of the land, but rather the battle for possession of Brick, the favorite son and the former athlete who has taken to drink. Like many Williams characters, Brick holds on to the fleeting sweet bird of youth and is absorbed by the past. He's especially detained by the memory of his friendship with Skipper. The play was evasive enough on the then-taboo sub-

SUDDENLY, LAST SUMMER (1959). As Catherine Holly

ject of homosexuality, but the movie is even more skittish, shrouding Brick's past in mystery and innuendo. As the movie tells it, Brick's problem is less with Skipper than with Big Daddy; this version of Brick is not so much a possible homosexual as he is an overage juvenile who's never had enough love and attention from his father. Once father and son have it out, Brick is cleansed: he can return to his wife's bed. Oversimplified, yes, but not bad if you must deal obliquely with what the play is really about.

In Hollywood, in 1958, the play's suggestions that Brick and Skipper had been lovers, that Brick is brooding because he feels responsible for his friend's suicide, and because he resents Maggie for having interfered, were clearly too explosive to handle. Williams was cowardly enough: *Cat on a Hot Tin Roof* is the kind of play in which being gay means going crazy or killing yourself in the last act. The movie approaches the subject even more gingerly than the original. All that's really clear is that Maggie has lost her husband's interest, and she has to fight fiercely to get it back.

In Williams' original third act, Maggie's victory is tentative. In the interest of giving the play a more upbeat and hence more popular ending, Elia Kazan (who directed the Broadway version) asked Williams to make Brick's return to wife and family more decisive. Insecure about the material anyway, Williams complied. Richard Brooks' movie uses the positive ending: Maggie gets Brick back, and Liz runs up the stairs, shouting joyfully in anticipation.

As always in Williams, it's the male who's cool and desirable, and the female who pants and clutches. Because she's a confirmed man-chaser, more pursuing than pursued, Liz is a congenial Williams heroine despite her beauty. But Maggie the Cat is not one of Williams' grotesque women; she's actually a steady, likable girl. The part requires the robust, open-hearted quality that Liz can supply when she's in the mood. Armed with a dry wit and an appreciation of fleshly pleasure, her Maggie is crafty, insistent, quick-tempered. Screaming at Brother Gooper's no-neck monsters, trading insults with Sister Woman, her cretinous antagonist, alternately cajoling and berating her errant husband, and talking from the heart to her sympathetic in-laws, Big Daddy and Big Mama, Liz is in full bloom, her lush Southern drawl charmingly rolled out for the occasion. Her sexiest screen mo-

SUDDENLY, LAST SUMMER (1959). With Katharine Hepburn

ment is when she cuddles up to Brick and tells him how nice he smells, how smooth his skin is: here is Taylor, the man-worshipper, at her most sultry.

Cat on a Hot Tin Roof is acted, as it must be, with combustible ensemble give-and-take. As Brick, Paul Newman, edgy and driven, gives the best performance of his career to date. Repeating his stage role, Burl Ives is an unbeatable Big Daddy. Judith Anderson (of all people)

makes a lusty Big Mama. And Jack Carson and Madeleine Sherwood are gloriously obnoxious as the couple everyone hates; Gooper and Mae and their squawling brood of no-neck monsters are Tennessee Williams' sly attack on heterosexual union.

Some audiences were puzzled by what happened "suddenly, last summer," but for Williams initiates, even in the movie version, the message was clear:

SUDDENLY, LAST SUMMER (1959). With Montgomery Clift

Sebastian was eaten alive by his boys. *Suddenly, Last Summer* is the playwright's ultimate homosexual fantasy. On an exotic island, a poet named Sebastian (Saint Sebastian, the martyr?) is crucified by the rough trade he has bought and dismissed like items on a menu.

Taylor is once again the Woman in the Way. As Catherine, voluptuous in a white bathing suit, she's the bait that attracts the boys. Does she know what she's being used for? Why does Sebastian use a woman as a come-on for homosexual encounters? Is he asking for trouble? Why, this summer, did he travel with his young cousin rather than his aging, imperious mother? Had she grown too old for her role as procuress? These are the play's mysteries and, one by one, in Williams' finest retrospective manner, they are answered. A convoluted mystery play, cunningly constructed, and

BUTTERFIELD 8 (1960). As Gloria Wandrous

acted with ferocious enthusiasm by Taylor and Katharine Hepburn as the arch-rivals for the cannibalized poet, *Suddenly, Last Summer* is homophile hijinx of a very high order. Florid and fevered, it is Williams' Southern Gothic at its ripest.

Her gay cousin used her as a procuress; her vindictive aunt threatens to have her lobotomized in order to stop her obscene babbling: Liz is again the unappreciated beauty. But she's also the abandoned innocent, a girl struggling to remember what happened to cousin Sebastian. Williams himself said she was "probably the finest raw talent on the Hollywood screen," but "it stretched [his] credulity to believe that such a hip doll as our Liz wouldn't know at once she was 'being used for something evil.' I think Liz would have dragged Sebastian home by his ears, and so saved them both from considerable embarrassment that summer. Echoing Williams' disbelief, Robert Hatch in *The Nation* thought that sane Liz is "obviously no more in need of brain surgery than she is of bust enhancement."°

She may be too "hip" to be fooled by what Sebastian was up

° *The Nation*, January 18, 1960.

to, but Liz tears into Williams' tumbling, turbulent prose with a vengeance. Catherine is the showiest and most fancily written part she ever had, and she misses none of its opportunities. From her opening scene in the asylum, pacing restlessly as she talks to the sympathetic Dr. Sugar (Montgomery Clift), to the final monologue, the orgasmic confession in which she finally arrives at the heart of the mystery, she acts with sustained urgency. Shrill, wide-eyed with remembered terror, she makes a mad dash at Williams' driving, purple, labyrinthine set speech. Her words are complemented by pictures—Joseph L. Mankiewicz opens up the play, and Williams' long one-act can take it, in a way that the more classically conceived *Cat on a Hot Tin Roof* cannot. Brisk cutting between the speaker and the events leading up to Sebastian's martyrdom heighten the already overheated atmosphere, and that monologue is Taylor's finest moment in the movies.

By the time *Butterfield 8* was released in 1960, Liz's public and movie image had changed; no longer the ethereal beauty or the determined Southern belle, she was the scarlet woman, a homewrecker who flaunted the rules by stealing Eddie from

Debbie. A woman who makes her own rules, Liz would seem to have been ideal casting for the role of a defiant call girl. But she didn't like the part: "The role they want me to play is little better than a prostitute," she protested. "Doing this picture gripes the hell out of me . . . It's too commercial, it's in bad taste. Everyone in it is crazy, mixed-up sick—except for the part Eddie plays." To please the squeamish star, some of the sex was cut, and the proceedings were generally "upgraded."

Curious behavior for Hollywood's misbehaving minx? Most actresses would relish the chance to play a B-girl, but Liz, remember, never coveted the showy roles, she never played whores or drunks or nuns or aspiring actresses. Her audience wanted to see her in sensational roles, but she preferred being proper.

Rewritten, the edge taken off, John O'Hara's Gloria Wandrous emerges somewhat undefined. The movie is so cautious that it's never clear exactly how the girl makes her living. She models, apparently, but does she get paid for sleeping with men, or does she sleep with men simply because she likes to? At the height of a family argument, Gloria confesses to her mother

that she was the slut of all time, but there is no evidence of this on screen. As in *The Last Time I Saw Paris*, Liz as girl-about-town is pallid, almost prissy. She doesn't have the freedom to portray amoral characters. She doesn't have the manic self-destructiveness the part requires. The script makes the character another of Taylor's tragic roles: Gloria Wandrous is a woman, mistreated by her man, who dies of unrequited love.

Like the conception of its heroine, the movie is infected with an enervating fuddy-duddy morality: once a sinner, the message goes, always a sinner. Deep down, this MGM Gloria feels that her indelible history of nights on the town has disqualified her for the likes of a respectable man. Self-convicted as a bad girl, she knows she's doomed.

Much more than the novel, the film (at Liz's prodding?) emphasizes Gloria's lust for respectability. Weston Liggett (Laurence Harvey), the wealthy Yale man, is her one big chance for graduation to the classy life of yachts and weekends in the country. It's as if the character wants to enter the world a younger Taylor so ably embodied in *A Place in the Sun*. After her fatal car crash, Liggett eulogizes her as a girl straining for respect-

BUTTERFIELD 8 (1960). With Eddie Fisher and Susan Oliver

ability: that's the movie's final statement about the girl at Butterfield 8, and it's a cheat. O'Hara's tough, precise, lovingly detailed novel has been transformed into Metro soap, a weepie about a sort of hooker with a yen for suburbia.

But even so, the movie was considered mildly daring at the time. Philip Hartung, in *Commonweal*, was disturbed to note that the movie "is so glossy and slick, it surrounds Gloria with an aura of glamor that almost obscures grim reality and the fact that she is sick, sick, sick."°

Liz thought it was dreadful, but she has appeared in worse. As MGM soap opera, as conventional romantic tragedy, the movie is flavorless (they updated O'Hara's evocatively etched Pro-

°Philip Hartung, *Commonweal*, November 11, 1960.

hibition-Depression New York to a blandly rendered contemporary Manhattan), but not impossible, and Liz is all right. In the last reel, she tries for tragic heightening, but the tears and the moral anguish are false to the dry-eyed O'Hara original. There are moments: the wordless opening scene, Taylor soiled and rumpled after a night with Liggett; Liz trading cracks with her mother's sardonic friend, and with her best friend's girlfriend; Liz convulsed in tears during an argument with her meek mother (Mildred Dunnock). Taylor and Laurence Harvey mix like oil and water, but her scenes with Eddie Fisher, who plays her platonic, disapproving buddy, are sturdy. Eddie gives her quiet support, the way Montgomery Clift always gave her strength on screen. Her big scene is her confession to Eddie about how she got started in the life: she was seduced by a house guest when she was thirteen, and she liked it (very wide-eyed, very shrill here), she has always *liked* it! (The confession scene is a

BUTTERFIELD 8 (1960). With Mildred Dunnock

With her "Oscar" for BUTTERFIELD 8

Taylor trademark during this period: in *Raintree County*, *Cat on a Hot Tin Roof*, *Suddenly, Last Summer*, and here, confessions dramatically lit and photographed are the focal points of her performances.)

She gets the character's self-pity, her sentimentality, her loneliness; she can do the smart answers, the head lifted in defiance. She plays, in short, with an authority that had deepened since *Giant*. In *Butterfield 8*, she dominates the way a star is supposed to dominate even if, finally, the role lacks definition.

The making of *Cleopatra* (1963), a publicist's dream that turned into a nightmare, was of course more theatrical than the final product. The on-screen romance cannot compete with the gleefully reported off-screen shenanigans among the Fishers and Burtons, with the colossal production miscalculations, with the star's near-death from pneumonia, with the news of the film's unprecedented cost. At the end of it, after the postponements and tantrums, after the backstage struggle for control of a big studio, after the changes in cast and director and the numerous script revisions, what emerged? A talky, intimate epic that nowhere suggests its absurd cost. A reasonably literate historical essay. A movie by Joseph L. Mankiewicz, which means that Cleopatra, Caesar, and Antony often sound like the bitchy actresses in *All About Eve*. There is always a lot of talk in Mankiewicz movies, and it's usually the kind of talk people make when they have drinks in their hands. The legendary trio make Manhattan cocktail party chatter, and it's all spiced with low-keyed sexual baiting. The movies can never make ancient people sound credible. What *did* Cleopatra talk like? Not, surely, the way Shakespeare or Shaw

THE QUEEN

suggested. So why not the dry, literate Hollywood-New York wit of Mankiewicz? "I've done nothing but rub you the wrong way," Cleo purrs, soon after rolling out of the rug; "I don't want to be rubbed by you at all, young lady," father Caesar chides her. Would this kind of banter have sounded more congenial, would it have been more appreciated, if *Cleopatra* had been a sensibly budgeted, non-scandal-ridden, unspectacular spectacle?

With Taylor cast as history's ultimate *femme fatale*, the scarlet woman of the ancient world, art certainly appeared to be reinforcing life. Before *Cleopatra*, the world had forgiven Liz for what she did to Debbie; her bout with death restored her to public favor (and even won her an Academy Award she didn't deserve). But the Burton affair was the last straw: obviously, the gossips concluded, she was a woman with no moral sense whatsoever. The world disapproved, but its eyes were riveted as it clucked its tongue. So far as art was concerned, the upshot was that no mere actress, no matter how

CLEOPATRA (1963). As the Queen of the Nile

CLEOPATRA (1963).
With Rex Harrison

CLEOPATRA (1963). With Richard Burton and Rex Harrison

high-priced or how luscious, could compete with the Roman scandals: Liz on screen in her Cleopatra gowns wasn't as tantalizing as the homewrecker whose antics were treated as if they had international consequence. Liz Taylor, modern minx, stole the spotlight from Cleopatra; she was grander in her own person than she was on screen as someone else.

It isn't big or intelligent or bold enough, but her interpretation of the Empress, scaled downward to accommodate her modest range, is not without some charm and some fire. Mankiewicz shaped the characterization to suit her; she isn't called upon to do anything she hadn't already done in contemporary settings. The movie follows her from the father-daughter romance with Caesar (Shaw territory) to the tempestuous man-woman contretemps with Antony (Shakespearean ground). The forty-million-dollar epic is constructed as a series of views of the Taylor woman from girlish, cuddly kitten, whining and purring her way into Caesar's bed, to ruler of the world, the woman who was too much for Antony.

Taylor is much better in the earlier section. As the cunning, nubile daughter to Caesar's wise papa, she's quite pleasing. She can handle the sardonic cracks and the little girl petulance. Though, of course, she hasn't Rex Harrison's Mayfair drawing room elegance, his courtly insouciance helps to shape her own performance.

She's expected to do much more "acting" as the womanly, passion-driven Queen, but she's more in control of the character when she's playing Caesar's pupil rather than Antony's teacher. Her high comedy exchanges with Harrison have quiet authority; her doomed romance with Burton never ignites. As a haughty, commanding Queen, Liz just isn't confident enough. The highest priced actress in history isn't too secure, and it shows. Whether berating Antony in the council chamber or slugging it out with him in her tomb, she lacks regal fire and authority.

Even more difficult for her was the depiction of Cleopatra as a crafty politician. The movie makes the character a kind of Eleanor Roosevelt captivated by the ideal of one-world unity. With a voice pitched to the intimacy of the bedroom rather than the formality of the council chamber, Liz is hardly at home as an ambitious stateswoman. She can respond to Cleopatra as a woman who gives up her life for love, but she cannot make her the brisk, ambitious executive the movie sometimes asks for. In her other movies, Liz's ambitions never exceeded the limits of romance, so it's no surprise to find her rather absent-minded when the Queen must attend to matters of state. "A Queen's days are full, but her nights are lonely," she coos to a sodden Antony. We can well envision how she'd like to spend those nights, but what was the official schedule like? The script, and Liz, offer few clues.

Mankiewicz said that their Cleopatra was not a vamp: "She was a highly complicated, intelligent woman who was carried to great heights in her ambition. Elizabeth has an understanding of this." The problem, of course, is that she doesn't: the girl who's

CLEOPATRA (1963). With Richard Burton

always had it so easy never played the role of an ambitious woman, and when she has to play a lady with the aspirations of a Crawford or a Hepburn, a woman who wants romance but who also wants to rule the world, she's caught short-handed. Neither life nor the movies have prepared her for such political appetite.

Taylor never suggests anything other than a contemporary siren. As Stanley Kauffman suggested, all she has to do is walk across the throne room in order to convert Alexandria into Beverly Hills. As everyone noted only too readily, the Taylor voice, lacking the range or the depth to suggest a mythic historical figure, is strictly contemporary.

Taylor's Cleopatra is a modern lady, shallow and saucy, cunning when it comes to being a female, not too bright when it's time for politics or war.

The star who was paid a cool million for her services at the height of her notoriety was not gently treated by the critics. "It pains one to reflect," wrote Archer Winsten in *The New York Post*, "that the Liz Taylor, so brutally overmatched here, who started her career with the perfection of *National Velvet* nineteen years ago, is over the edge. *Cleopatra* proves an expensive way to demonstrate it." Kinder, *Newsweek* conceded that she is "not the worst actress in the world. She can do an acceptable love scene, and she has a modest gift for delivering witty dialogue." Brendan Gill in *The New Yorker* offered the fairest and wisest assessment, claiming that Liz is "less an actress by now than a great natural wonder, like Niagara or the Alps, and it was right of the director . . . to deal with her as the thing she has become—the most famous woman of her time, and probably of all time, who, perfectly made up, her nakedness picked out in cloth of gold (and the camera never failing, from scene to scene, to make obeisance to that justly celebrated bosom), is set pacing from bed to bath and from Caesar to Mark Antony not as the embodiment of a dim, ancient queen but as, quite literally, a living doll, at once so sexy and so modish that her historical predecessor, seeing her, might easily have died not from the sting of an asp but from the sting of envy."°

°Brendan Gill, *The New Yorker*, June 23, 1963.

On her television special, "Elizabeth Taylor in London," October 6, 1963

THE V.I.P.s (1963). With Richard Burton

Not only in *Cleopatra* but in her next two films as well, *The VIPs* (1963) and *The Sandpiper* (1965), Taylor was more the world-famous celebrity and less the conscientious actress than at any other time in her career. The three movies exploit the public's fantasy of what the lovers must be like: tempestuous, as in *Cleopatra*; bickering, on the verge of separation, as in *The*

VIPs; illicit lovers, defying the moral norms, as in *The Sandpiper.* As the ancient Queen of the Nile, as modern day *grande dame*, or as a hippie artist, Taylor is Taylor, hemmed in by her spectacular fame. The international celebrity, the world's most famous lover, takes over from the burgeoning actress of the Fifties, and Taylor walks through the movies as the fabled beauty she'd become rather than the high-strung Southern belle she had been before Rome.

After *Cleopatra*, the Burtons claim they weren't in demand. The publicity backfired, and their soggy on-screen romance didn't help. The scarcity of offers surely accounts for their choice of *The VIPs*, an old-fashioned programmer that made an oddly appropriate follow-up to *Cleopatra*. With a craftsmanlike script by Terrence Rattigan and sturdy old line direction by Anthony Asquith, the movie is a throwback to an earlier tradition in moviemaking: it's *Grand Hotel* MGM. The VIP lounge of the London Airport is analogous to Vicki Baum's hostelry as a background for the unfolding of multiple, interlocking personal dramas.

The Burtons are a prodigally wealthy couple, and their grand entrance, via helicopter, has the panache befitting the reigning King and Queen of Movieland. Liz once again is the neglected wife, comforting herself with a lover. When he's threatened by his wife's departure, the husband, who has given diamonds instead of affection, shows he cares. Liz is adamant, however; she wants him to suffer. Only when Burton decides to kill himself and she finds out does she realize he needs her. The couple are reunited (without ever really having been separated): despite their great wealth, despite his previous indifference, despite her temptations (Louis Jourdan is waiting in the wings), they are respectable, conventional people after all.

The inevitable reconciliation is reached by means of improbable coincidences—the machinations of Rattigan's plot are enough to make Scribe blush. But the details hardly matter. The Burtons behave like stars, he shamelessly working his speeches as though they were Shakespearean arias, she being very dignified and remote, on her best ladylike behavior after *Cleopatra*. At the end, she has a tearful scene that gives her the kind of torrential emoting she had practiced since *National Velvet* and *The Courage of Lassie*; for the rest, she's cool and serene, her face undisturbed by normal human

THE V.I.P.s (1963). With Louis Jourdan

expression. Playing an instigator of male insecurity, she's not, for a change, altogether sympathetic here. In *The New York Times* Bosley Crowther noted that she has "a strange sort of icy detachment—almost cruelty—toward both men."

The Burtons by no means dominate the movie, and again, as in *Cleopatra*, the chemistry isn't quite there. He has that deep sonorous voice he's so immensely proud of; she's working with her high, little-girl breathiness. He's stage-trained, an emphatic classical actor. She's movie-trained, skillful at not giving the camera more than it can absorb. His rant and her movie-fashioned subtlety do not mix; often they don't seem to be occupying the same movie space. Burton may be one of the finest classical actors of his generation, but as a movie actor in movie star material, he's no match for his wife. When they have combustible scripts, with equally weighted parts, as in *Who's Afraid of Virginia Woolf?* and *The Taming of the Shrew*, they are truly responsive to each other. Their renditions of Albee's and Shakespeare's embattled lovers are intelligent tandem performances. But in their other five movies together, the disparity between the Old Vic and MGM

THE V.I.P.s (1963). As Frances Andros

Forties shows—and not to the advantage of the former.

In *The VIPs* Burton gives too much and Taylor just barely gives enough, but it doesn't matter. It's Old Hollywood fustian and a big-cast movie like this is only as good as its supporting actors. Maggie Smith, as a plain secretary with a crush on her boss, and Margaret Rutherford,

THE SANDPIPER (1965). With Richard Burton

as a daffy, indigent duchess, stole the show and got all the reviews. (Rutherford won an Academy Award as Best Supporting Actress.)

The Sandpiper keeps the Burtons more occupied. Burton thought he was working on more trash, and he took the money and ran, but Liz liked the script, and it's easy to see why. Playing an unmarried woman who lives with her son exactly the way she wants to live, in harmony with the California coast, Liz, for once, gets to talk about ideas: her character is a proto-Women's Libber proclaiming the joys of independence and self-expression. Taylor is no Jane Fonda, alight with radical fervor, but the role does express something of herself; it lets us see a side of her that differs from the standard screen Taylor. Here she's a New Woman, free and wise, who teaches a thing or two to a rigid Episcopal clergyman. The film's symbol is the sandpiper with a broken wing which she offers as proof that every creature should be allowed to fly free.

We know too much about her to believe her as a hippie, and her earnest performance is further undermined by her impossibly slick make-up and wardrobe: no self-respecting woman who thinks she's a Kerouac beatnik would dress so fashionably or live in such a colossally elegant cabin in the woods. The foolish star packaging aside, Liz is game, announcing her character's faintly leftist ideas with all the conviction and sincerity she can muster.

The character's broad humanistic philosophy—her objections to organized religion and to formal schooling, her advocacy of free love and her celebration of the naturalness of physical love—are, oddly enough, at the film's center. (*Newsweek* complained that the script, by Dalton

THE SANDPIPER (1965). With Richard Burton

Trumbo and Michael Wilson, provides "the least drama possible, transfixed as it is by copybook maxims on individualism, cosmogony, religion, society and love.") The story that interrupts the character's ongoing declarations about life is the old number of a minister tempted by a beautiful woman. Bombarded by the artist's charms, the man succumbs, only to depart at the end, weighed down by guilt and vowing to seeking the way of repentance and purification.

The movie's morality is thus a mingling of the old and the new. The affair is consummated, as it would not have been in the days of the Hays Office, but the straying minister must be ashamed of his adultery. Feeling himself unworthy of his pure wife (Eva Marie Saint) and of his job, he leaves in search of a new ministry. Judith Christ, in the *New York Herald Tribune*, noticed that "the moral seems to be that there's nothing like a round of adultery to make a clergyman develop a social conscience." More disturbed by the implications of the movie's shifty morality, Bosley Crowther in the *Times* remarked that it is "a slick and sympathetic sanction of the practice of free love—or, at least, of an illicit union that is supposedly justified by naturalness."

The movie plays it both ways, admiring the woman's freedom and righteous self-justification, but making the minister pay dearly for his indulgence in forbidden fruit. It's an old Hollywood romance trying to masquerade as a love story in the hip modern manner. The attempt to appease a mass audience's sense of propriety—titillation overlaid with conventional piety—robs the movie of any genuine liberal politics, but what can you expect of a big budget romance with the Burtons?

Burton's prude is impossible and he plays him in a stiff oratorical manner, as if he's deadening himself to the pain of it all, but Taylor's character almost approaches being a real rebel with ideas. The movie exploits the public image of her as a defier of conventions, but the role also gives her a chance to sound reasonably articulate about matters other than love. She'd never had a pseudo-Shavian part like this before and under Vincente Minnelli's graceful guidance, she is sweet if not entirely convincing.

Her hair grayed, her face lined and puffy, her frame padded with her own fat, her high little voice lowered to a scratchy, whiskey-soaked middle bass, Taylor whooped it up in the stunt of her career. Stimulated by Albee's lacerating wit, and responding to Mike Nichols' detailed direction like the good student she had always been, Liz overcame the celebrity jinx and proved, once again, that there was an actress underneath the star. There are chinks—moments when you can feel the strain, can see she's "acting"—but on the whole it's a spectacular job.

The convention has been to cast the rumpled heroine of *Who's Afraid of Virginia Woolf?* with a brash, masculine actress. Uta Hagen, Mercedes McCambridge, and Kate Reid played her on Broadway. Brash, yes, but hardly masculine, Taylor brings some needed shading and softening to Albee's astringent, deeply misogynistic portrait. A sentimental actress, Taylor eases her character toward the play's final reconciliation when, after George has destroyed their imaginary child, Martha capitulates, giving in to her need for her husband and looking forward to a bruised but salvageable married life.

But Taylor's Martha is no

THE SHREW

milksop. She enters into the gameplaying with high spirits; her delight in attacking and humiliating George is as keen as her dependence on him. The Albee bitch is brushed, then, with Taylor tenderness, and the upbeat ending, Albee's show-wise gimmick to send the audience home happy, is therefore made plausible. On stage, you didn't believe that Hagen's strident, tough Martha would ever say yes to Arthur Hill's meek George, but you are convinced that Taylor would knuckle under to Burton's quiet, absolute authority.

Who's Afraid of Virginia Woolf? is about the taming of the shrew, and the part, except for the age hurdle, is Taylor-made, exploiting both her spoiled child bitchiness and her inevitable vulnerability. A twitchy woman fighting to save her marriage, Martha certainly has cross-references to the archetypal Taylor of Maggie the Cat.

Albee's classical structure—one set, no time breaks, his emphasis on corruscating wit and characterization as opposed to narrative, his purely literary and symbolic use of an imaginary child to suggest the incompleteness of George and Martha's marriage—gives the material a decidedly theatrical flavoring. And yet *Who's Afraid of Virginia Woolf?* is perhaps the best *movie* in which Taylor ever appeared. Nichols' direction not only has pace and tension, but he avoids the confined, static look of a prestige play transferred to an alien medium. Blocked for the camera rather than the proscenium, tautly edited, and photographed in a rich, grainy black and white, the action has movie-like rhythm and texture. The stars in a superb tandem per-

WHO'S AFRAID OF VIRGINIA WOOLF? (1966). As Martha

WHO'S AFRAID OF VIRGINIA WOOLF? (1966). With Richard Burton

formance, George Segal and Sandy Dennis as the dreary young academic couple whose late-night visit catalyzes George and Martha's "show," Nichols, Albee—the movie was a triumph for them all.

What did *Virginia Woolf* do for Elizabeth Taylor? It compen-

sated for *Cleopatra*. She won her second Oscar, this time for what happened *on* screen rather than off. Her success as the dowdy, middle-aged bitch, in fact, was the inspiration for her new movie image: the fishwife that she'd been accused of turning Cleopatra into became her new movie

113

WHO'S AFRAID OF VIRGINIA WOOLF? (1966) With Richard Burton,
George Segal and Sandy Dennis

persona. The bulk of her post-*Virginia Woolf* work (*The Taming of the Shrew, Reflections in a Golden Eye, Boom!, Secret Ceremony, X Y and Zee,* and *Hammersmith Is Out*) represents variations on the Albee matron. *Virginia Woolf* released the Taylor vulgarity and emphasized the qualities that had been in the Taylor iconography all along: the sharp tongue, the temper, the relish for a good fight.

After *Virginia Woolf*, she is usually the blowsy, gutsy harridan who cusses up a storm, gives full rein to her appetites (food and men), and delights in exchanging insults with both sexes. In this post-mid-career mannerist phase, Taylor, no longer the lovely ingenue, is frequently sloppy, but she isn't dull. Discovering new ways of relating to her audience, she's much freer than she ever was before. She's no longer MGM's most dutiful student; she's up there on her own, using (and sometimes abusing) the personality she's always had in reserve. In most of these later movies, she's an overripe, overweight dame who doesn't care and who seems to be having a lot of fun, enjoying being a movie star for perhaps the first time.

The Taylor shrew, on the whole, has been a happy evolu-

tion. As they approach or pass middle age, many stars have no place to go. They can't continue to play the kinds of parts that made them stars in the first place, and yet they are unwilling to play roles suitable to their maturity. Sometimes, like Katharine Hepburn and Bette Davis, they become ghoulish parodies of their younger selves, aping the mannerisms that made them famous. Davis in *The Anniversary* or Hepburn in *The Lion in Winter* are cut-rate versions of the real thing, merchandising cheap and distorted reproductions of themselves. Some stars, like Debbie Reynolds or Doris Day, who are unwilling to act their age and who can't find a suitable replacement for their ingenue image, stop making movies altogether.

Her discreditors would contend that Taylor never had that much personality to play around with. But *Virginia Woolf* released her from bondage, and since then the Taylor image has been punchier, the personality broader and more brightly colored. The image kept pace with the expanding waistline, the predilection for gaudy outfits (toreador pants and enormous mou-mous), teased piled hair, inch-thick make-up, diamonds. The delicate little girl-woman of *National Velvet* became a great bawd, a remnant of a garish, splashy, madcap Hollywood that was.

Ironically, though, as her personality expanded and flared, as she gained new confidence, creating for the first time something of the spectacularly scaled personality that legendary movie stars are supposed to have, her box office record was less stable. At the time of *Virginia Woolf*, Taylor could claim that she had never been in a film that lost money. After *Virginia Woolf*, however, her name above the title did not guarantee a return investment. She became, in fact, something of a coterie star doing a Taylor "shtick" for her chuckling fans.

In *The Taming of the Shrew*, *The Comedians*, and *Reflections in a Golden Eye*, Taylor is still the bankable star appearing in prestige properties. The real loss of popularity began in 1968, with *Boom!* and *Secret Ceremony*. In these two films and in *X Y and Zee* and *Hammersmith Is Out*, Taylor became quirkier and more mannered and self-indulgent, and the movies themselves were lopsided curiosities. Choosing less commercial material (nobody could ever have thought that *Secret Ceremony* or *Hammersmith Is Out* would make money), she was no longer the star who could command a million. Cutting up in campy vehicles, she was becoming somewhat passé. Hard-core Elizabethans were enchanted, but the mass public that had gaped in *Cat on a Hot Tin Roof* or *Butterfield 8* or *Cleopatra* stayed away, no longer very interested in the fat lady with the diamonds who made odd-ball movies.

Except for *Hammersmith Is Out*, though, which is a trashy send-up of its stars, the vehicles Taylor clowned about in had respectable credentials. *The Comedians* had a script by Graham Greene, adapting from his own novel. Directed by John Huston, *Reflections in a Golden Eye* was based on the splendid novella by Carson McCullers. *Boom!* and *Secret Ceremony* were directed by Joseph Losey, and *Boom!* was based on *The Milk Train Doesn't Stop Here Any More*, a two-time Broadway flop by Tennessee Williams. Reuniting Taylor with George Stevens, *The Only Game in Town* was based on a play by

*ANNE OF THE THOUSAND DAYS
(1970). As an extra*

Frank D. Gilroy, who had won a Pulitzer Prize for *The Subject was Roses*. And though it was shabby, *X Y and Zee* was written *for* Taylor by Edna O'Brien, a highly regarded English novelist.

The Taming of the Shrew, *Reflections in a Golden Eye*, and *The Comedians* did modestly well. *Boom!* and *Secret Ceremony* performed dismally everywhere except France (where Joseph Losey is a first-level *auteur*). *The Only Game in Town* opened in New York in neighborhood theatres, the first time a Taylor movie had been so casually showcased since *The Girl Who Had Everything*. *X Y and Zee* was considered something of a comeback movie, but box-offices outside the big cities were not besieged. *Hammersmith Is Out* was hardly distributed at all. (In addition, the Burtons made two movies purely for Art; they never expected a return on *Dr. Faustus* or *Under Milk Wood*, and they never got one.)

Some of these (*The Comedians*, *Hammersmith Is Out*, *The Only Game in Town*) just didn't work. All of the films were commercial disappointments. But in almost all of them Taylor blossoms as a screen personality if not as a serious actress. As a bawd, a shrew, a campy actress exaggerating her mannerisms and burlesquing her femininity, she is enjoyable to watch.

Only twice does she depart from the new bitch mold, and only in these films, *The Comedians* and *The Only Game in Town*, is she lacklustre. (Her cameos in *Dr. Faustus* and *Under Milk Wood* hardly count. In Burton's thoroughly mistaken, Walt Disney-colored rendition of Marlowe's tragedy, Liz is Helen of Troy and a number of other high-class historical ladies. She has no dialogue, but she turns up periodically in preposterous overdress. Her every gesture convicts her of non-royalty. In *Under Milk Wood*, as the town whore lolling in bed with Peter O'Toole, she's a lush embodiment of Dylan Thomas sensuality, and her lilting Welsh accent is lovely.)

In *The Comedians* (1967), standing around on the sidelines in what amounts to a state of unemployment, she's featureless. (Not even a try at a thick German accent livens her up.) As the mistress of one of Graham Greene's typical burnt-out cases, Taylor is altogether incidental to the political intrigue. An ambassador's restless wife, the mother of a whining child and the mistress of an empty shell of a man, she is given no real character to work with; she's just another Taylor woman who's unlucky in love. Surprisingly, the too frequent love scenes with Burton are the clumsiest of her career; in this one, she doesn't even kiss very well. The Burtons, appearing as the Burtons, are in the way. "Aside from them," *Newsweek* asserted, "as if anything could be aside from them, *The Comedians* might have been a good film."

Graham Greene's novel,

DR. FAUSTUS (1968). As Helen of Troy

which mixes adultery with dictatorship in Papa Doc Duvalier's Haiti, is not very good in the first place. It reads like the scenario for a glossy politics-cum-romance thriller. The political intrigue in exotic settings has some interest, but Liz' dialogue is sudsy: "My dear, my darling, don't torture yourself": "Sometimes I don't think we can go on as we are." On his own, playing the proprietor of a ramshackle hotel who

DR. FAUSTUS (1968). With Richard Burton

unwillingly gets involved in revolutionary activity, Burton is sensible and his scenes with Alec Guinness as a bogus colonel and enterprising soldier of fortune and with Paul Ford and Lillian Gish as two impossibly innocent American do-gooders, have a fine, sharp edge.

Taylor has more to do, but she is no happier, in *The Only Game in Town* (1970). Cast against type (she's playing one of her rare working class girls), she's a dancer in a Las Vegas chorus line who lives in a plastic little apartment and watches old movies on late night television. The ambiance doesn't jell for Liz; we've heard too much about the diamonds and the yachts and the enormous household staff to believe her in such modest circumstances. The *Morning Telegraph* noted rather sagely that "Big Liz can't escape her reality and neither can we. It might have seemed a grand idea to get her for the role. Imagine Elizabeth Taylor as a lonely, luckless girl. The irony of it all. But this switch in circumstance is moron-

THE COMEDIANS (1967). As Martha Pinada

THE COMEDIANS (1967). With Richard Burton, James Earl Jones, Alec Guinness, and Peter Ustinov

THE ONLY GAME IN TOWN (1970). With Warren Beatty

ic, not ironic, for she is never less than Big Liz . . . For her the role of Fran (how's that for a plain, everyday name) is a living lie, almost a mockery of the people who never really do quite make it in life."

Frank D. Gilroy's slender, sentimental script is about practically nothing at all. A girl meets a guy (Warren Beatty), they go to bed, they part, they get together again. He has a gambling problem, and she's engaged to an older married man who keeps promising to get a divorce. The gambler is a ladies' man; slick and smooth, he cons his way into the girl's bed and then into her heart.

In a lightweight romantic comedy-drama like this, the

charm is everything. As the gambler, Warren Beatty has it; as the bruised, lonely, overage chorus girl, Liz doesn't. Her off-screen aura works *against* the role, just as Beatty's image as her fickle lover works beautifully *for* the character. Liz tries, though, and as Pauline Kael said in *The New Yorker:* "She has a sweetness, and despite her rather shapeless look, a touching quality of frailty (like some of the women stars of an earlier era, as she gets older she begins to have a defenseless air about her)," but she is really too old for this sort of thing, and far too heavy and matronly to pass as a chorus girl kicking up her heels every night to earn a meagre living.

Beatty transforms the material, making it seem much sharper and brighter than it is. His brash, cocky charm, his deft comic timing, his light seductive voice turn the proverbial sow's purse into silk. When she catches Beatty's light style, Taylor is pleasant, but when she goes weepy, when Stevens encourages her to play the dramatic actress with at-

THE ONLY GAME IN TOWN (1970). With Warren Beatty

REFLECTIONS IN A GOLDEN EYE (1967). With Marlon Brando

tendant stammers and blinks and helpless hand gestures, she misplaces the character.

As uninvolved ambassador's wife or as plain Fran, Taylor isn't much to look at, but her six bawd parts, in *The Taming of the Shrew, Reflections in a Golden Eye, Boom!, Secret Ceremony, X Y and Zee,* and *Hammer-* *smith Is Out,* are spectacular if not always disciplined.

Containing her one quiet, non-stunt-like performance in this late, rococo phase of her career, *Reflections in a Golden Eye* stands apart from the others. Her character here is a reminder of the Fifties Southern belles rather than the post-*Virginia Woolf*

Taylor shrew at full blast. She plays a flighty lady who takes a lover because her husband,'s interest is elsewhere, and the role is a droll mixture of Taylor cruelty (she taunts her husband) and Taylor softness (she's all compassionate understanding for her lover, who's burdened with a psychotic wife).

A Southern spitfire whose type she's played before, the character is a child-woman hooked on sex. Significantly, though, the role calls on the essential Taylor sanity, for she and her lover (Brian Keith) are the only sexually adjusted characters on an army post overrun with Carson McCullers misfits. Taylor's husband (Marlon Brando) is a guilt-ridden closet homosexual, preoccupied with physical fitness and with a brooding soldier who rides his horse in the nude and whose sexual tension is released by sitting surreptitiously at the foot of Taylor's bed. Brian Keith's wife (Julie Harris) spends her time spinning fantasies with an effeminate Filipino houseboy. Taylor and Keith are the "straights," aloof from the others' coiled, tortured sexuality.

REFLECTIONS IN A GOLDEN EYE (1967). With Julie Harris

REFLECTIONS IN A GOLDEN EYE (1967). With Marlon Brando

Lush Southern Gothic, shown originally in a tinted version that suppressed the color to a golden monochrome, the movie didn't get the attention it deserved. Popular audiences felt alienated; except for Taylor and Keith, the characters were too odd to feed mass fantasies. Even though her own character doesn't have the baroque coloration of her parts in *Boom!* or *Hammersmith Is Out*, *Reflections in a Golden Eye* is the first of the downbeat, off-center Taylor movies.

Deftly approximating McCullers' cool, ironic tone, the film is quietly directed by John Huston and superlatively underplayed. Taylor's Leonora Penderton is caricature (an almost-parody of her Williams belles), but she's never noisy. In tune with the movie's low-keyed tension, Taylor works quietly. We often catch isolated words and phrases of her non-stop chit-chat; we hear her girlish laughter or her raucous titters in the background. Hers is a decorative rather than central character, but she's both amusing and nasty in a performance that mixes the Taylor laugh with the Taylor sneer. In her most charming scene, she describes, in breathless, mouth-watering detail, the refreshments for her officers' party.

THE TAMING OF THE SHREW (1967). As Kate

129

THE TAMING OF THE SHREW (1967). With Richard Burton

THE TAMING OF THE SHREW (1967). With Richard Burton

Her few scenes with Brando (a great, unheralded performance) crackle with sexual antagonism. They are colossally mismatched: he's an inverted intellectual, she's a featherbrain. Fighting back when she's rejected, Taylor taunts the major in her sauciest wench manner, flourishing the pulchritude and playing up the role of the vulgar hussy that offends his prissy morality. When he describes the purity of the life of men among men, Taylor, the eternally excluded woman, flashes looks that could kill. Spiced with bitter innuendo and juicy sarcasm, their scenes have the electricity that Taylor and Burton don't always manage.

A low profile performance in a moody, low slung movie, Taylor's silly minx is only an intimation of the full-dress bawd she contributes to *The Taming of the Shrew, Boom!, Secret Ceremony, X Y and Zee*, and *Hammersmith Is Out*.

Her Kate in Shakespeare's comedy (1967) is the first post-*Virginia Woolf* harpie. In an interview about the film, Liz said that Shakespeare's shrew was "totally different" from Albee's. But her description of Kate is

BOOM! *(1968). With Richard Burton*

BOOM! (1968). As Mrs. Flora Goforth

also an apt description of her Martha: "She's a wild little animal wanting to be caught. She's madly on the defensive all the time. She's the eternal female. She wants to acquiesce but doesn't know how. She adores Petruchio but you know she's never going to be tamed. You know at the end that their life will be wild, but it will be a ball." Her Kate, like her Martha, is thus another instance of art imitating life. In both movies, the Burtons are playing out the kind of rocky romance the *Photoplay* public always thought they had. (Liz confided to David Frost that a good fight is "the greatest exercise in marital togetherness.")

Shakespeare's play was a follow-up to Albee's. Shouting, clawing, mugging, running, slugging, the Burtons kept up the lively show they had put on in *Virginia Woolf*, serving Shakespeare as snappily as they had served Albee. Their *Shrew*, in fact, is the most joyous Shakespeare ever put on film, a nonstop romp that cuts speeches and characters from the original, but that retains its lusty spirit and its sexual wisdom all the same. Zeffirelli's *mise-en-scène* and the melodious score are wonderfully lush, the supporting cast is agile, and, at the center, are the Bur-

tons, the most popular stars in the world (at the time), proving themselves worthy of the deluxe packaging.

Burton, of course, has the easier time with the Shakespearean metre, but Taylor meets him in energy if not in the sophistication of her line readings. Together, they give us a battle royal, "a salty salvo in the war between the sexes" in which, *Time* punned, Taylor makes Kate "the ideal bawd of Avon." The performance has shape, Taylor taking Kate deftly from minx to matron. At the beginning she is all animal high spirits; impetuous, unleashed—she is the sort of untamed gal who needs a nononsense man to appreciate her and to keep her in line. When Petruchio is finished with her, she's calmed and socialized. A properly behaved member of the community, she dutifully recites her ode to the manly man.

Boom! (1968), a year later, is another version of the Taylor hellcat, but this time critics and audiences weren't buying the vaudevillian routine. Based on Tennessee Williams' unhinged play, the movie is sumptuous to look at (a pink villa overlooking the Mediterranean upstages the Burtons), but the dramatic conflict is minimal. An aging voluptuary is courted and "saved" by a mystic young man, a life-poet who has a Mediterranean-wide reputation for visiting rich ladies on death's doorstep. A typical Williams fantasy, in which sex, death, and transcendence are uneasily linked, the movie is even less focused than its source, and for those unfamiliar with Williams, *Boom!* does not make much sense.

As the world's richest lady, dying of tuberculosis, a raunchy ex-Follies queen who is the veteran of numerous marriages and affairs, Liz is too *zaftig* and robust—and much too young. (The role was patterned, none too flatteringly, on Tallulah Bankhead, and Tallulah even played it in its second Broadway outing.) Appearance and age aside, however, Liz as Tallulah enjoys herself: she clearly relishes the character's vulgarity and imperious stupidity. Riding high on her new persona, Taylor puts on a whale of a show, sharpening her claws with Noel Coward as The Witch of Capri, crucifying Italian as she tries to order dinner for her house guest, reciting florid Williams monologues about catastrophic marriages. As she proved before, she is a vivid Williams actress.

Here, in her rococo phase, she meets Williams head on in his. Depending on flamboyant personal signature, they're neither of them at their best. The play marked the beginning of Williams' popular decline and her strung-out work here marked the beginning of hers.

Joseph Losey, a director noted for his *mise-en-scene* and particularly his preoccupation with houses (*The Servant, Secret Ceremony*) is more concerned with background than foreground, and he doesn't give Taylor the kind of disciplined direction she needs. Unlike her work in *Virginia Woolf*, her performance lacks shading. Ranting and sneering with uncorseted ebullience, she here begins her bid for the world's most beautiful successor to Tallulah.

Trashy as she is, however, she's far more appropriate than Burton, who is cruelly miscast as Chris Flanders, a Williams angel of mercy who soothes the transition between life and death for rich, edgy old women. Williams thought of the character as a young, golden Adonis, a tantalizing blend of innocence and worldliness. Burton would hardly be anyone's first choice for such a role; Tab Hunter, who played it opposite Tallulah, was much more suitable.

Taylor's vaudevillian strut appears in a quite different context in *Secret Ceremony* (1968).

SECRET CEREMONY (1968). With Mia Farrow

Here, she is a tired two-bit hustler, or as Liz put it, with typical finesse, "I play a dikey prostitute in this one." For the first time in her career, she plays a character who doesn't like men, a woman battered by a life on the streets who has come to regard men as her natural enemies. Given her animosity, this is a Taylor triangle with a twist: her character fights a burly Robert Mitchum for possession of waif-like Mia Farrow.

A psychological thriller in the Pirandellian mold, the movie depicts the fantasy world created by the young girl and the older

prostitute. The girl thinks Taylor is her mother, and she brings her home to her once resplendent, now faintly decayed London town house. The two women, locked away from the world outside, enact a "secret ceremony" in which fantasy mingles with and reshapes reality, and Taylor is only too willing to exchange her role of streetwalker for that of the mad girl's rich mama.

Secret Ceremony is a murky, arty movie—a far cry from the MGM Main Street Americana that provided the backbone of Taylor's career—and her role is tricky, complex:

SECRET CEREMONY (1968). With Mia Farrow

X Y AND ZEE (1972). As Zee

the ratty hooker must become a *grande dame*. Flustered in the face of a pivoting of illusion and reality, Taylor uses her *Virginia Woolf* number for a role that needs subtler shadings. (Roger Greenspun, in *The New York Times*, commented that her misreading of every line approaches sublimity.)

Secret Ceremony looks terrific (Joseph Losey again going to work on a magnificent dream-like house), but this is no triumph for Liz. The role pushes against Taylor stereotype, but she isn't elastic enough to transcend her new-found image.

By the time of *X Y and Zee* and *Hammersmith Is Out*, it no longer matters. Both films have no reason for being other than to provide a showcase for Taylor's persona as "the blowziest scarlet woman in a Mexican movie," Pauline Kael wrote in *The New*

X Y AND ZEE (1972). With Michael Caine

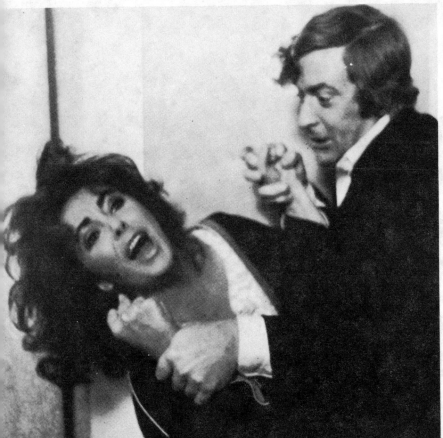

HAMMERSMITH IS OUT (1973). With Beau Bridges

Yorker. In *X Y and Zee* (1972), Liz is the dark heroine, a passionate woman who listens to blaring rock; Susannah York is the misty-eyed fair heroine, all prissy decorum, who listens to dignified classical music. Paunchy Michael Caine is the man between. The contest is merely an excuse for Liz, as the randy wife of a straying husband, to bask in the vulgarity she has such contagious fun with. Like Maggie the Cat, Liz-Zee is determined to ensnare her man, even going so far as to seduce her rival. (Taylor's embrace of Susannah York is awfully tentative, altogether lacking the fervor of her attentions to Lassie or Paul

Newman or Montgomery Clift.)

Part "Suzy Says" peek at jet set shenanigans, part lugubrious soap opera, the movie is a blatant and hollow confection. Two hours of relentless bitching by Liz, it's a valentine to her fans, a good-natured send-up of her earth mother, sex goddess image.

Pauline Kael suggested that the movie marks "the coming out" of Elizabeth Taylor: "a world-famous woman chang[es] status and, I think, maybe get[s] in touch with the audience in a new egalitarian way. Her range has become even smaller . . . she's not enough of an actress to get by with the bruised and hurting bit. She's got to be active and brassy and bold; she's best when she lets her gift for mimicry and for movie-colony sluttiness roll out . . . The aging beauty has discovered in herself a gutsy, unrestrained spirit that knocks two very fine performers right off the screen . . . She's Beverly Hills Chaucerian and that's as high and low as you can get."°

Hammersmith Is Out (1973) is the dumbest, most disorganized movie Liz ever made. As a vehicle, it's on a par with Crawford wielding an axe or Davis sporting a fright wig. *Hammer-*

°Pauline Kael, *The New Yorker*, February 12, 1972.

smith is the Burtons on holiday; the slightly over-the-hill stars are making a home movie for their fans in which they good-naturedly yet magisterially burlesque themselves. (For starters, as they're trying to swipe a car at a drive-in, they listen attentively to the sudsy dialogue from a Cleopatra-like epic.)

In a scruffy blonde wig, Liz plays a hashslinger in a roadside diner. The lady, a cartoon character named Jimmie Jean Jackson, is a gold-digger who latches onto Billy Breedlove (Beau Bridges), a hillbilly attendant at the local nut house who's been promised wealth and power by Hammersmith (Burton), the star inmate. The movie is a modern reduction of the Faust myth: Billy Breedlove is the insatiable quester; Hammersmith the oily Mephistopheles; and Jimmie Jean Jackson the bargain basement Helen. Tagging along with the boys, Jimmie Jean moves up in the world; before long, the rube waitress is hobnobbing with the international royalty.

"Gee—we could even have things we don't want—wow!" Liz drools, in anticipation of the treasures Hammersmith promises. The Burtons are obviously having fun spoofing their reputations as vulgar big-spenders; the

142

DIVORCE HIS/DIVORCE HERS (1973). With Richard Burton in the television play

diamonds and the yachts hover on the edge of the movie. Liz camps it up in a series of blackout skits that burlesque her career. Jimmie Jean is another Taylor woman in the way who has trouble holding her man. (The hillbilly moron tires of her, presumably because she's so vacant, and so she has a child by the devil.) Liz has never been less sure of a character, and her approach changes almost from scene to scene. Now she has a Southern accent, now she doesn't. Here she's a real dumb Dora; there she's a wise woman who would give up all her wealth to be a mother. She stammers. She squints and flashes those famous violet eyes. Running through the Taylor repertoire, she titters, guffaws, sneers, pouts, smirks, and frowns. She's vulnerable, bitchy, womanly, grasping, both hard and soft.

NIGHT WATCH (1973). With Laurence Harvey

It's the Taylor show, served up in harum-scarum, helter-skelter fashion. "Say something dirty," a fat man pleads with her, as they're sprawled on an enormous bed like two hippos in heat; "Peepee," she squeaks, after a Methody pause. "I'm the biggest mother of them all," she announces, grabbing her stom- ach as if she's just been shot. Shrill and outrageous, the film is a black comedy designed to titil- late the hard-core Taylor buff.

Worlds removed from the classy literary packages of the Fifties or the million dollar show- cases of the Sixties, *X Y and Zee* and *Hammersmith Is Out* are strictly coterie movies, splashy vehicles for an aging celluloid queen. Liz takes over, assaulting her audience with her gaudy modern rendition of the Wife of Bath, and her high-flying, rococo self-parody is reason enough for seeing both these ornery, lopsided programmers.

The ads for *Night Watch* (1973) announced that no one would be seated during the last twenty minutes, and this was a blunt reminder that Elizabeth Taylor had never before appeared in a lower-case genre picture. Confined for the most part to glossy romantic dramas, her career had been conspicuously aloof from urban crime thrillers, mysteries, adventures, war stories, musicals—yet here was a potboiler with a trick ending to stain the record.

The film is cluttered with standard Gothic paraphernalia: a spooky abandoned house, ghosts (perhaps real, perhaps imagined), peals of rolling thunder, prominently displayed kitchen knives. Lucille Fletcher's artificial Broadway whodunit, cluttered with red herrings, is a step down even from *Hammersmith Is Out*, and in the attemptedly eerie finale, as she gleefully knifes her husband and his mistress, poor Liz looks alarmingly like Baby Jane or Sweet Charlotte.

In these decidedly diminished circumstances, Liz is nonetheless in familiar territory, playing yet another rich, unoccupied, unwanted wife. She's not a shrew this time, though, she's a cool, crafty lady who pretends to be unhinged, concocting an elaborate display of madness— she "sees" dead bodies in the house next door—by which she hopes to entrap her straying husband and her faithless best friend. There are clues throughout, but we aren't fully alerted to her masquerade until the end. This scorned wife set on ultimate revenge is a tricky, double-edged role, then, and like so much of her recent work, Taylor's performance is spotty, subtly insinuating in one scene, curiously off form, uncommunicative, in the next.

It's not a flattering part: she plays a woman who has been rejected by two husbands. And the character's "acting" emphasizes Liz's recent penchant for doing a lot of "acting" herself. Her show of neurosis, in fact, is too mannered and actressy to be consistently convincing. She's best when, at the beginning, she's the serene upper-class wife and again, at the end, when she lashes out directly at her antagonists. In the last reel, when we're onto her and can see the calm de-

NIGHT WATCH (1973). As Ellen Wheeler

liberation beneath the affected hysterics, she's especially appealing. Even as a knife-wielding murderess, Liz knows how to woo her audience. But hopefully this unmistakably second-rate genre movie is a mere digression from the "official" career and not a gloomy presentiment of garish roles in hokey horror vehicles.

As a child, she was an angel with the face of a woman. As an ingenue, she had the heart of a flirt in the body of a goddess. Southern belles brought her movie maturity. Hollywood bitches gave her confidence and freedom. Elizabeth Taylor hasn't stayed still, then; from saintly animal lover to poor little rich girl to young woman of passion to vulgar Old Hollywood strumpet, she's forged ahead, modulating, expanding, emphasizing, and spoofing her image. An instinctive if not an inspired actress, a performer with manner, temperament, and individuality, she hasn't stopped working for thirty years. The little girl who grew up in front of the whole country, the movie star with the most publicized private life in Hollywood history, the Queen of Tinsel Town, is indisputably one of the last of her kind.

BIBLIOGRAPHY

Agee, James. *Agee on Film*. Beacon Press, Boston, 1958.

Allan, John B. *Elizabeth Taylor: A Fascinating Story of America's Most Talented Actress and the World's Most Beautiful Woman*. Monarch Books, Derby, Connecticut, 1961.

Burton, Philip. *Early Doors. My Life and the Theatre*. The Dial Press, New York, 1969.

Brodsky, Jack, and Nathan Weiss. *The Cleopatra Papers. A Private Correspondence*. Simon & Schuster, New York, 1963.

Cottrell, John, and Fergus Cashin. *Richard Burton. Very Close Up*. Prentice-Hall, Inc., Englewood Cliffs, New Jersey, 1971.

Elkin, Stanley. "Miss Taylor and Family: An Outside View," *Esquire*, November, 1964.

Essoe, Gabe. "Elizabeth Taylor's Career," *Films in Review*, August-September, 1970.

Latham, Aaron. *Crazy Sundays. F. Scott Fitzgerald in Hollywood*. Viking, New York, 1970.

Rice, Cy. *Cleopatra in Mink*. Popular Library, New York, 1962.

Ringgold, Gene. "Elizabeth Taylor's Career," *Film Careers*, Fall, 1963.

Schickel, Richard. *The Stars*. The Dial Press, New York, 1962.

Sheed, Wilfrid. "Burton and Taylor Must Go," *Esquire*, October, 1968.

Taylor, Elizabeth. *Elizabeth Taylor*. Harper & Row, New York, 1964.

Waterbury, Ruth. *Elizabeth Taylor. Her Life, Her Loves, Her Future*. Appleton-Century, New York, 1964.

THE FILMS OF ELIZABETH TAYLOR

The director's name follows the release date. Sp indicates screenplay and b/o indicates based on.

1. THERE'S ONE BORN EVERY MINUTE. Universal, 1942. *Harold Young*. Sp: Robert B. Hunt and Brenda Weisberg. Cast: Hugh Herbert, Tom Brown, Peggy Moran, Catherine Doucet, Carl "Alfalfa" Switzer.

2. LASSIE COME HOME. MGM, 1943. *Fred M. Wilcox*. Sp: Hugo Butler, b/o novel by Eric Knight. Cast: Roddy McDowall, Donald Crisp, Dame May Whitty, Edmund Gwenn, Elsa Lanchester.

3. JANE EYRE. Twentieth Century-Fox, 1944. *Robert Stevenson*. Sp: Aldous Huxley, John Houseman, and Mr. Stevenson, b/o book by Charlotte Bronte. Cast: Orson Welles, Joan Fontaine, Margaret O'Brien, Peggy Ann Garner, Sara Allgood, Ethel Griffies, Mae Marsh.

4. WHITE CLIFFS OF DOVER. MGM, 1944. *Clarence Brown*. Sp: Claudine West, Jan Lustig, and George Froeschel, b/o poem "The White Cliffs" by Alice Duer Miller. Cast: Irene Dunne, Alan Marshal, Roddy McDowall, Van Johnson, Dame May Whitty, Gladys Cooper.

5. NATIONAL VELVET. MGM, 1944. *Clarence Brown*. Sp: Theodore Reeves and Helen Deutsch, b/o novel by Enid Bagnold. Cast: Mickey Rooney, Donald Crisp, Anne Revere, Angela Lansbury.

6. COURAGE OF LASSIE. MGM, 1946. *Fred M. Wilcox*. Sp: Lionel Houser. Cast: Frank Morgan, Tom Drake, Selena Royle, George Cleveland.

7. CYNTHIA. MGM, 1947. *Robert Z. Leonard*. Sp: Harold Buchman and Charles Kaufman, b/o play *The Rich Full Life* by Vina Delmar. Cast: George Murphy, S.Z. Sakall, Mary Astor, Gene Lockhart, Spring Byington, James Lydon.

8. LIFE WITH FATHER. WB, 1947. *Michael Curtiz*. Sp: Donald Ogden Stewart, b/o play by Howard Lindsay and Russel Crouse, b/o writing of the late Clarence Day, Jr. Cast: William Powell, Irene Dunne, Edmund Gwenn, ZaSu Pitts, James Lydon.

9. A DATE WITH JUDY. MGM, 1948. *Richard Thorpe*. Sp: Dorothy Cooper and Dorothy Kingsley, b/o characters created by Aleen Leslie. Cast: Wallace Beery, Jane Powell, Carmen Miranda, Xavier Cugat, Robert Stack, Scotty Beckett, Selena Royle, Leon Ames.

10. JULIA MISBEHAVES. MGM, 1948. *Jack Conway*. Sp: William Ludwig, Harry Ruskin, and Arthur Wimperis, from a Gina Kaus and Monckton Hoffe adaptation of the novel *The Nutmeg Tree* by Margery Sharp. Cast: Greer Garson, Walter Pidgeon, Peter Lawford, Cesar Romero, Lucile Watson, Mary Boland, Veda Ann Borg.

11. LITTLE WOMEN. MGM, 1949. *Mervyn LeRoy*. Sp: Andrew Solt, Sarah Y. Mason and Victor Heerman, b/o novel by Louisa May Alcott. Cast: June Allyson, Peter Lawford, Margaret O'Brien, Janet Leigh, Rossano Brazzi, Mary Astor.

12. CONSPIRATOR. MGM, 1950. *Victor Saville*. Sp: Sally Benson and Gerald Fairlie, b/o novel by Humphrey Slater. Cast: Robert Taylor, Robert Flemyng, Honor Blackman, Thora Hird, Wilfred Hyde-White.

13. THE BIG HANGOVER. MGM, 1950. *Norman Krasna*. Sp: Mr. Krasna. Cast: Van Johnson, Percy Waram, Leon Ames, Edgar Buchanan, Gene Lockhart, Selena Royle, Rosemary DeCamp.

14. FATHER OF THE BRIDE. MGM, 1950. *Vincente Minnelli*. Sp: Frances Goodrich and Albert Hackett, b/o novel by Edward Streeter. Cast: Spencer Tracy, Joan Bennett, Don Taylor, Billie Burke, Moroni Olsen, Leo G. Carroll, Rusty Tamblyn.

15. A PLACE IN THE SUN. Paramount, 1951. *George Stevens*. Sp: Michael Wilson and Harry Brown, b/o novel *An American Tragedy* by Theodore Dreiser and the play by Patrick Kearney. Cast: Shelley Winters, Montgomery Clift, Keefe Brasselle, Raymond Burr.

16. FATHER'S LITTLE DIVIDEND. MGM, 1951. *Vincente Minnelli*. Sp: Albert Hackett and Frances Goodrich, b/o characters created by Edward Streeter. Cast: Spencer Tracy, Joan Bennett, Billie Burke, Moroni Olsen, Rusty Tamblyn.

17. LOVE IS BETTER THAN EVER. MGM, 1952. *Stanley Donen*. Sp: Ruth Brooks Flippen. Cast: Larry Parks, Josephine Hutchinson, Tom Tully, Ann Doran, Elinor Donohue, Kathleen Freeman.

18. IVANHOE. MGM, 1952. *Richard Thorpe*. Sp: Noel Langley, adaptation by Aeneas MacKenzie, b/o novel by Sir Walter Scott. Cast: Robert Taylor, George Sanders, Emlyn Williams, Joan Fontaine, Finlay Currie, Felix Aylmer.

19. THE GIRL WHO HAD EVERYTHING. MGM, 1953. *Richard Thorpe*. Sp: Art Cohn, b/o novel *A Free Soul* by Adela Rogers St. Johns. Cast: William Powell, Gig Young, Fernando Lamas, James Whitmore.

20. RHAPSODY. MGM, 1954. *Charles Vidor*. Sp: Fay and Michael Kanin, adapted by Ruth and Augustus Goetz, from the novel *Maurice Guest* by Henry Handel Richardson. Cast: Vittorio Gassman, John Ericson, Louis Calhern, Michael Chekhov.

21. ELEPHANT WALK. Paramount, 1954. *William Dieterle*. Sp: John Lee Mahin, b/o novel by Robert Standish. Cast: Dana Andrews, Peter Finch, Abraham Sofaer, Mylee Haulani.

22. BEAU BRUMMELL. MGM, 1954. *Curtis Bernhardt*. Sp: Karl Tunberg, b/o play by Clyde Fitch. Cast: Stewart Granger, Peter Ustinov, Rosemary Harris, James Donald, Robert Morley.

23. THE LAST TIME I SAW PARIS. MGM, 1954. *Richard Brooks*. Sp: Julius J. and Philip G. Epstein and Mr. Brooks, b/o short story "Babylon Revisited" by F. Scott Fitzgerald. Cast: Van Johnson, Walter Pidgeon, Donna Reed, Eva Gabor.

24. GIANT. WB, 1956. *George Stevens*. Sp: Fred Guiol and Ivan Moffat, b/o novel by Edna Ferber. Cast: Rock Hudson, James Dean, Carroll Baker, Jane Withers, Mercedes McCambridge, Chill Wills, Sal Mineo, Dennis Hopper.

25. RAINTREE COUNTY. MGM, 1957. *Edward Dymtryk*. Sp: Millard Kaufman, b/o novel by Ross Lockridge, Jr. Cast: Montgomery Clift, Eva Marie Saint, Nigel Patrick, Lee Marvin, Rod Taylor, Jarma Lewis, Tom Drake.

26. CAT ON A HOT TIN ROOF. MGM, 1958. *Richard Brooks*. Sp: James Poe and Mr. Brooks, b/o play by Tennessee Williams. Cast: Paul Newman, Burl Ives, Judith Anderson, Jack Carson, Madeleine Sherwood.

27. SUDDENLY, LAST SUMMER. Columbia, 1959. *Joseph L. Mankiewicz*. Sp: Tennessee Williams and Gore Vidal, adapted from the play by Mr. Williams. Cast: Katharine Hepburn, Montgomery Clift, Mercedes McCambridge.

28. BUTTERFIELD 8. MGM, 1960. *Daniel Mann*. Sp: Charles Schnee, b/o novel by John O'Hara. Cast: Laurence Harvey, Eddie Fisher, Mildred Dunnock, Betty Field, Dina Merrill.

29. CLEOPATRA. Twentieth-Century Fox, 1963. *Joseph L. Mankiewicz*. Sp: Ranald MacDougall, Sidney Buchman, and Mr. Mankiewicz, b/o histories by Plutarch, Suetonius, Appian, other ancient sources, and *The Life and Times of Cleopatra*, by C.M. Franzero. Cast: Rex Harrison, Richard Burton, Roddy McDowall.

30. THE V.I.P.s. MGM, 1963. *Anthony Asquith.* Sp: Terence Rattigan. Cast: Richard Burton, Louis Jourdan, Maggie Smith, Margaret Rutherford, Orson Welles, Rod Taylor, Linda Christian.

31. THE SANDPIPER. MGM, 1965. *Vincente Minnelli.* Sp: Dalton Trumbo and Michael Wilson, b/o original story by Martin Ransohoff. Cast: Richard Burton, Eva Marie Saint, Robert Webber.

32. WHO'S AFRAID OF VIRGINIA WOOLF? WB, 1966. *Mike Nichols.* Sp: Ernest Lehman, b/o play by Edward Albee. Cast: Richard Burton, George Segal, Sandy Dennis.

33. THE TAMING OF THE SHREW. Columbia, 1967. *Franco Zeffirelli.* Sp: Paul Dehn, Suso Cecchi d'Amico and Mr. Zeffirelli, adapted from play by William Shakespeare. Cast: Richard Burton, Michael Hordern, Cyril Cusack, Alan Webb, Michael York.

34. REFLECTIONS IN A GOLDEN EYE. WB, 1967. *John Huston.* Sp: Chapman Mortimer and Gladys Hill, b/o novel by Carson McCullers. Cast: Marlon Brando, Brian Keith, Robert Forster, Julie Harris, Zorro David.

35. THE COMEDIANS. MGM, 1967. *Peter Glenville.* Sp: Graham Greene, b/o his novel. Cast: Richard Burton, Alec Guinness, Peter Ustinov, Roscoe Lee Browne, Gloria Foster, Paul Ford, Lillian Gish.

36. DOCTOR FAUSTUS. Columbia, 1968. *Richard Burton and Nevill Coghill.* Sp: adapted by Mr. Coghill from the play by Christopher Marlowe. Cast: Richard Burton, Andreas Teuber.

37. BOOM! Universal, 1968. *Joseph Losey.* Sp: Tennessee Williams, b/o his play *The Milk Train Doesn't Stop Here Any More.* Cast: Richard Burton, Noel Coward, Joanna Shimkus, Michael Dunn, Howard Taylor.

38. SECRET CEREMONY. Universal, 1968. *Joseph Losey*. Sp: George Tabori, b/o short story by Marco Denevi. Cast: Mia Farrow, Robert Mitchum.

39. THE ONLY GAME IN TOWN. Twentieth-Century Fox, 1970. *George Stevens*. Sp: Frank D. Gilroy, b/o his play. Cast: Warren Beatty.

40. X Y AND ZEE. Columbia, 1972. *Brian G. Hutton*. Sp: Edna O'Brien. Cast: Michael Caine, Susannah York, Margaret Leighton.

41. HAMMERSMITH IS OUT. J. Cornelius Crean Films, 1972. *Peter Ustinov*. Sp: Stanford Whitmore. Cast: Richard Burton, Peter Ustinov, Beau Bridges, Leon Ames, George Raft.

42. UNDER MILK WOOD. Altura Films, 1972. *Andrew Sinclair*. Sp: Mr. Sinclair, b/o play by Dylan Thomas. Cast: Richard Burton, Peter O'Toole, Vivien Merchant, Glynis Johns, Ann Beach.

43. DIVORCE HIS, DIVORCE HERS. ABC-TV, February 6 and 7, 1973. *Waris Hussein*. Sp: John Hopkins. Cast: Richard Burton, Gabriele Ferzetti, Barry Foster, Carrie Nye.

44. NIGHT WATCH. Avco-Embassy, 1973. *Brian G. Hutton*. Sp: Tony Williamson, b/o play by Lucille Fletcher. Cast: Laurence Harvey, Billie Whitelaw, Bill Dean, Robert Lang.

45. ASH WEDNESDAY. A Sagittarius Production released by Paramount, 1973. *Larry Peerce*. Sp: Jean-Claude Tramont. Cast: Henry Fonda, Helmut Berger, Keith Baxter.

46. IDENTIKIT (THE DRIVER'S SEAT). Rizzoli-DeLaurentiis, 1974. *Giuseppe Patroni Griffi*. b/o novel by Muriel Spark. Cast: Guido Manmari, Ian Bannen, Luigi Squarizina.

INDEX

155

ABOUT THE AUTHOR

Foster Hirsch has written on films, theatre, and books for numerous publications, including *The Nation*, *The New Leader*, *The New York Times*, *The Village Voice*, *Film Quarterly*, *Film Heritage*, *Film Comment*, *Commonweal*, *The Educational Theatre Journal*, *Shakespeare Quarterly*, and *Cinema*. He is the author of critical studies of the plays of Tennessee Williams and George Kelly.

ABOUT THE EDITOR

Ted Sennett is the author of *Warner Brothers Presents*, a survey of the great Warners films of the thirties and forties, and of *Lunatics and Lovers*, on the years of the "screwball" movie comedy. He has also written about films for magazines and newspapers. A publishing executive, he lives in New Jersey with his wife and three children.